more

more

The Four Dimensions of Intimacy with God

MARILYN N. ANDERES

Chosen

Grand Rapids, Michigan

Published by Chosen Books
a division of Baker Publishing Group
P.O. Box 6287, Grand Rapids, MI 49516-6287

Second printing, November 2006

Printed in the United States of America

Library of Congress Cataloging-in-Publication Data
Anderes, Marilyn N.
   More : the four dimensions of intimacy with God / Marilyn N. Anderes.
     p.   cm.
   Includes bibliographical references.
   ISBN 10: 0-8007-9407-9 (pbk.)
   ISBN 978-0-8007-9407-1 (pbk.)
   1. Spirituality. I. Title.
BV4501.3.A48 2006
248.4—dc22   2005036732

This book is dedicated to our grandchildren:
Hannah Joy Adams
Kyle Thomas Adams
John Robert Anderes IV ("J.J.")
Jamie Ellen Anderes
Jackson Mark Anderes
Alicia Kaye Anderes

I pray that the God of the "immeasurably more than all" will make you mighty in spirit. I pray that no one will "look down on you because you are young, but [that you will] set an example for the believers in speech, in life, in love, in faith and in purity" (1 Timothy 4:12).

Contents

Acknowledgments

*H*eartfelt thanks to the many people who have made a difference in my journey with the Master. Gratefulness goes to God for Joy and Bob Boeck, who prayed my husband and me into the Kingdom. For George and Carol Anderson, who cared for us over decades and taught us truths from the Scripture. Thanks to Susan Bailey and Linda Harrington, who are loving accountability partners. To Grace "Tikki" Jefferson and Jean Fleming, who have prayed this book into being. To shield bearers like Sandy Ahalt, godly role models like Faye Short and those who watch after my soul, like John Metcalfe. Thanks to Merrilea Greenawalt, Betty Lewis and Penny Henderson, quiet and faithful cheerleaders, and to ministry partners like Elaine Snow and Kelly Willie. Gratefulness goes to those I have mentored and led in retreats. You have made my life rich, teaching me much. Thanks also for the encouragement of Patty and Lewis McDorman, Tim and Cindy Carson and Rich and Andrea Yates. Gratefulness goes to God for my editors, Jane Campbell and Ann Weinheimer, for believing in me and becoming my friends.

Above all, I thank my husband, John, and our children, Joy and Tom Adams, John and Karen Anderes, and Mark and Lisa Anderes. God has used you to continue His transforming work in me. Watching you keep in step with the Lord and receiving your steadfast love for this flawed one never ceases to amaze me. You all are immeasurably more than all I could ever have asked or imagined.

May God receive the honor and glory.

Introduction

A wise Hasidic Jewish saying declares an important truth: "It is not within our power to place the divine teachings directly into someone else's heart. All that we can do is place them on the surface of the heart so that when the heart breaks, they drop in."

My guess is that you have been devoted to growing in the Lord for many years. Through salvation by faith in Jesus Christ you are rooted and established in God's love, but perhaps you think that your growth depends on how much you know and how much you can accomplish. In my own experience, that was when the Holy Spirit humbled me and taught me to surrender to His touch. When my heart broke in repentance, everything that was stacked on top—all the Bible verses learned by rote, all the Christian activity and all the information logged—fell in. No longer was I puffed up with knowledge. I was being changed from the inside out. Transformed. The process of being changed by the One who never changes continues and I find myself bumping into God's love at every turn. And so can you.

God's love has many dimensions. It is wide and long and high and deep. He beckons us to know Him, to stop defending the images we project onto Him and to come close. We can bow to the mystery and stop thinking we have God all figured out. And, as we do, we grow. If your heart resonates with this challenge, then the time is now and this book is for you. Join me in the journey of growing spiritually in every dimension. Study questions at the end of each chapter will guide you in a personal quest or group challenge to ponder your own situation more thoroughly.

Just picture the width of God's love. Perhaps you have been admiring His banquet table, wide-eyed and nibbling an hors d'oeuvre or two, when His invitation rings out: *Join the feast*. You look across the wide table, loaded with the richest of fare. No mere morsels for you! Can you believe it? He loves you so much that you are invited to fulfill your longing for more, even if you do not feel worthy to do so.

God's love is long, too. Perhaps you have the desire to be a spiritual marathoner, to run the race well, but you cannot seem to get your feet untangled as you stumble over obstacles on your way. Yet He challenges you: *Stay the course*. As you surrender entanglements and expectations, you begin to realize that you can do it *with* Him just as your spirit can be set free to run with abandon *toward* Him.

Come up higher. There's more. God smiles His plea. He is drawing you close. You know that the mountain is there to be climbed—others have gone before you. Moses scaled Sinai. Abraham climbed Moriah. Jesus took the challenge of Calvary and made the way for us all. And if climbing a mountain is too daunting at first, we can, like Zacchaeus, start by just climbing a tree. The result is the same. By going higher they all saw God.

God's love has another dimension. It is deep as a river. And He is calling, *Take the plunge.* Perhaps you yearn to immerse yourself in the depths of God. Nothing held back. And you can be the first to shout to those around you, "Come on in! The water's fine."

One of the exciting things about this pilgrimage is that it was never meant to be traveled alone. A banquet is not a banquet with just a few. A race is not a race with only one. The steepest mountains are best scaled with someone to help hold your ropes. And most of us have been taught from childhood never to swim alone. We need each other to do this right. And we require the power of the Holy Spirit.

Yes, you and I can know more of Him. We can *become* more like Him. We can grow in all the dimensions of God's love. Wider. Longer. Higher. Deeper. Humility, brokenness and surrender bring certain transformation. Are you up for the challenge?

My prayer for you as you read this book echoes Paul's heart:

> I pray that you, being rooted and established in love, may have power, together with all the saints, to grasp how wide and long and high and deep is the love of Christ, and to know this love that surpasses knowledge—that you may be filled to the measure of all the fullness of God.
>
> Ephesians 3:17–19

Now that is growth in intimacy!

wider

The Banquet Table

He has taken me to the banquet hall, and his banner over me is love.

Song of Songs 2:4

1

God's Invitation

There must be more than this." That is the heart cry of many. It is what settled the American West and planted footsteps of an earthling on the moon. The problem comes in knowing what *more* looks like and how to get there. The Creator programmed us with a hunger and thirst for more of Him, so apart from Him, adventure, power, knowledge, riches and even serving Him will not satisfy. Isaiah asked: "Why spend money on what is not bread, and your labor on what does not satisfy?" (Isaiah 55:2). Why indeed?

It is not more of the same that fulfills. It is more of Him. And in the pilgrimage to more of Him we realize that, amazingly, He longs for more of us. Consider Eugene Peterson's rendering of Psalm 14:2: "GOD sticks his head out of heaven. He looks around. He's looking for someone not stupid—one man, even, God-expectant, just one God-ready woman" (MESSAGE). *More* is spelled *s-u-r-r-e-n-d-e-r*.

John the Baptist got it. He said: "He [Jesus] must become greater; I must become less" (John 3:30).

Years ago when our then four-year-old son, John, wanted more of me, he would spin me around and put his little hands on my face and say in as serious a voice as he could muster, "Mommy, point your face at me." His pathos never failed to give me a smile. What followed was predictable. He would invite me to stop and taste a cookie or to answer a question burning in his heart or to look at treasures in his hands. Usually they were rocks or worms.

One day I came upon Psalm 27:8. David says: "When You said, 'Seek My face,' my heart said to You, 'Your face, O LORD, I shall seek'" (NASB). It was as if God had spun me around and put His big hands on my face. *Marilyn, point your face at Me.*

When God prods you to come and grow in the four dimensions of intimacy with Him, it translates into "Point your face at Me." When He bids you to explore the width, length, height and depth of His love, when He invites you to His feast, His race, His mountain and His river, He is repeating Himself yet again. *Point your face at Me.* Then He invites you to a place of R & R—a grown-up cookie break. He answers your questions even before you form them and He shows you treasures in His Word.

My prayer is that this book woos you—pushes you, if need be—to point your face at Him. I invite you to start now with the feast. The hall is ready. The table is wider than you can imagine and it is laden with every delicacy. He says: *Come to the banquet. All the seats are places of honor and I promise the richest of foods. Allow Me to wash your feet before you take your place at the table. I long to lavish My love on you.*

If the mail carrier brought such an invitation to you, would you think it was delivered to the wrong address?

The most sumptuous feasts I have ever attended are hosted by NASA. They are the annual Goddard Memorial Dinners in Washington, D.C., with impeccable preparations, lavish surroundings and honored guests. There are always lots of people in fancy clothes, rich food and wine, music, dancing and laughter.

God offers even more extravagance. He is looking for a bride who has "made herself ready. Fine linen, bright and clean, was given her to wear" (Revelation 19:7–8). His preparations are extraordinary. "Everything is now ready," He proclaims (Luke 14:17). The table presents "the richest of fare" (Isaiah 55:2). This is "a banquet of aged wine—the best of meats and the finest of wines" (Isaiah 25:6). There are many guests. "Blessed are those who are invited" (Revelation 19:9). "You will be honored in the presence of all your fellow guests" (Luke 14:10). The host takes great delight in you and rejoices over you with singing (see Zephaniah 3:17). It is a time "to celebrate and be glad" (Luke 15:32).

That would be an invitation difficult to ignore and yet I bet you do it all the time. I do. Not long ago I read the following sentence in a noted Christian women's magazine: "One reason many are disappointed with life is they keep praying for a gourmet meal instead of just giving thanks for their daily bread." Though I understand the intended message, I would say this instead: "One reason many are disappointed with life is they settle for fallen crumbs instead of reveling in the richest of fare."

God longs for us to be hungry and thirsty for Him. He wants us to grow spiritually so that He can show us the wonder of a banquet only He can offer. Calvin Miller, in *Loving God Up Close* (Warner Faith, 2004), contends that "we are too hungry for the eternal to feel satisfied with the contrived and the contemporary." God invites consistently:

"All is ready." But Satan plays on our hunger and taunts us to turn stones into bread. So we settle for lesser menus. The enemy's forgery offers food that is hard, stale and tasteless. We believe his lies.

Perhaps you feel that you cannot go to the feast because you do not look right; you do not have the proper clothing. Or perhaps you are afraid because you do not know how to dance. Or maybe you have not finished all your expected chores and the time to twirl freely is frankly just . . . not yet.

Perhaps you have a desire to move ahead with God, to grow spiritually, but as you labor faithfully—stacking Bible memory verse cards, outlining biblical success formulas, counting participants at programs you direct—not much progress is apparent. Is it possible that you look alive but you know something is amiss?

If you feel that way, you are not alone. Countless others who know Jesus are experiencing the same thing. They are "doing church" and not encountering the God of the church. It is as if they are asleep, napping for years like Rip Van Winkle while the invitation to receive *more* gathers dust.

That reminds me of the preschooler who fell out of bed in the middle of the night. When his mother ran to comfort him, she asked the frightened little boy what had happened. He said, "I don't know. I guess I fell asleep too close to where I got in."

That is what some of us did. We fell asleep too close to where we got into the faith. That is why we long for more.

I want to tell you the story of a young woman named Karen. She knows there is a feast and she is now convinced of God's desire for her to come and enjoy His blessings there. But it was not always that way.

Accepting the Invitation

In the middle of a women's conference I had the privilege of leading, the participants enjoyed a wonderful worship time. I stood in the rear of the room swept up with enthusiasm for God. Karen happened to be in my line of vision, framed on all sides by like-minded friends.

She raised her hands in praise. It was lavish worship, but I had not noticed until that moment that her hands were deformed. One hand did not have the normal number of fingers and the other was twisted and gnarled. Scars indicated previous surgeries. I gasped, realizing that toes had been grafted onto her hands in the place of some fingers. I was blessed by her expression of unashamed, uninhibited love for God.

After the worship I went to Karen to share how her response to God had touched me. She started to cry and said, "That is the first time I've ever done that. For forty years at church I have hidden my hands beneath a hat on my lap. This weekend God convinced me that He loves me, and if He can love 'deformed me' then I decided I'd give my all to Him. I had to raise my hands. And I don't care who sees."

The story doesn't end there. At one point during the weekend, door prizes were offered and my friend received one of the gift envelopes. Later she shared her new gift with me. My face fell. It was a certificate for a manicure. But Karen was giggling. She shook my shoulders. "You really don't get this. Yesterday that would have been my response. But today I'm free. God has a great sense of humor. I'm going to give this gift away."

And that is still not the end of the story. Karen moved to a new state and began attending a new church. She was looking for ways to serve the Lord when a notice in the church bulletin caught her eye. It was a plea for ministry help and called for skills she had. Today she is signing for the hearing challenged, and they understand what she is saying to them—even though she has fewer fingers than most.

In Ephesians 3:20, just two verses after the declaration about the width, length, height and depth of God's love, Paul says that our God "is able to do immeasurably more than all we ask or imagine, according to his power that is at work within us." Notice the stages in this statement. First is what we ask for and next is what we imagine could happen. But God does immeasurably more. And sometimes even more than that.

Karen had asked God often: "How could you love me with these misshapen hands?" She even imagined that one day God would heal her physically. She knew He could. But God did more. He healed her heart and freed her to raise her hands, giving Him passionate love in return. Then He did immeasurably more. As Karen opened the gift certificate, He took her shame. She rejoiced with Him. And then He did even more than all. She now serves God . . . with her hands.

The feast began for Karen. She was convinced. God's banner over her is love.

In Romans 5:5 Paul tells us that "God has poured out his love into our hearts by the Holy Spirit, whom he has given us." What a gift! And it is not just a tiny bit; it is a pouring out. In the original Greek this pouring is rendered as "gushing out" or "rushing headlong in our direction." And did you notice? It is past tense. That means He poured out His love long ago (see Romans 5:8) and has just been waiting for us to be convinced.

Being convinced of God's love is of critical importance because when we know that He loves us, we are free to love

Him back. We are also at liberty to love others with His love. Second Corinthians 5:14 says that His "love compels us." Have you ever watched someone trying to relate to another whose allegiance is in question? It is awkward at best. When we are sure God loves us we are free and safe to love other people. Even enemies. Even the unlovely.

God always welcomes a humble, contrite heart, but without the certainty of His love, we are shy to approach the Holy One with our own unholiness. The banquet hall is a scary place unless we are sure of a loving welcome.

Like Karen, I needed to be persuaded of God's love for me. I mouthed the phrase *God is love* many times, but I was never sure of it personally. I knew I was saved by grace, but, in reality, I lived by performance. So I made a lateral move when I first came to Christ because that was how I coped in my formative years. I thought, *If I do well, I will be loved more, but if I mess up, I'm in trouble.*

In that regard, I found somewhat of a kindred spirit in the person of God's servant Job. I have not endured anything close to the losses this man suffered, but I think we are alike in many ways. And I suspect you are, too.

Let's look at his story of surrender to God's love.

Lessons from Job

Job was a man who tried to do all the "right" things. He loved God, and he was respected for his godliness—God Himself called Job blameless and upright—but he had not really connected with the divine. He looked good on the outside, but he had not fully surrendered his life. Job had to let go of his expectations, his own way, words, reputation and control—even his own concept of God—in order to come to the feast. When he surrendered everything that kept his

23

heart from being humble, then true repentance came and his eyes and ears were opened to the wonders of God.

The biblical account puts Job's life under the microscope. Consider this testimony from Job's friend Eliphaz: "Think how you have instructed many, how you have strengthened feeble hands. Your words have supported those who stumbled; you have strengthened faltering knees" (Job 4:3–4). This sounds good at the outset, but sometimes even well-meaning Christian friends do not help us in the process of surrender. Ultimately Eliphaz encouraged Job to find hope in himself and in what he had done: "Should not your piety be your confidence and your blameless ways your hope?" (Job 4:6).

Such is the flattery of friends: "What do you mean that something is missing? What more growth could you want with God? Think how you have helped people. You have given comfort and support to so many." It is easy to become inflated by such words, to buoy ourselves up with glowing assessments. Job did.

> "But [God] knows the way that I take; when he has tested me, I will come forth as gold. My feet have closely followed his steps; I have kept to his way without turning aside. I have not departed from the commands of his lips; I have treasured the words of his mouth more than my daily bread."
>
> Job 23:10–12

I have been there. Have you been there, too? You are probably a woman of the Word. You make some right responses (see Job 1:20–22) and you make some wrong responses (see Job 9:33–35). And God has most likely used you in the lives of other followers of Jesus. We entertain assessments that we are "blameless," "upright," "supportive" and even "gold," but still we know in the depths of our hearts that we are not broken and surrendered. Words sound hollow when compared with the transforming touch of God the Father, the Son and the Holy Spirit and the spiritual growth that it brings.

Job 42:1–6 makes it all clear:

> Then Job replied to the LORD: "I know that you can do all things; no plan of yours can be thwarted. You asked, 'Who is this that obscures my counsel without knowledge?' Surely I spoke of things I did not understand, things too wonderful for me to know. You said, 'Listen now, and I will speak; I will question you, and you shall answer me.' My ears had heard of you but now my eyes have seen you. Therefore I despise myself and repent in dust and ashes."

These verses represent Job's surrendered response. His losses prompted a quest for more. Previously Elihu spoke true words of his friend: "Job speaks without knowledge; his words lack insight" (Job 34:35). And in Job 38:2–3 God thundered these words: "Who is this that darkens my counsel with words without knowledge? Brace yourself like a man; I will question you, and you shall answer me." God repeated this statement in Job 40:7.

Remember the Hasidic Jewish saying mentioned in the introduction to this book? "It is not within our power to place the divine teachings directly into someone else's heart. All that we can do is place them on the surface of the heart so that when the heart breaks, they drop in." God had spoken the identical words before, but now Job's heart was broken and humble, ready to receive.

Job finally understood the difference between worldly sorrow and godly sorrow. Second Corinthians 7:10 says: "Godly sorrow brings repentance that leads to salvation and leaves no regret, but worldly sorrow brings death." Godly sorrow realizes that God's heart is hurt not just because you suffered a loss but because He longs for intimacy with you.

Instead of "woe is me" over his loss of health, wealth and family, Job finally confessed, "My ears had heard of you, but now my eyes have seen you." The result? Repentance. The accompanying action? Surrender. The final outcome? Transformation, intimacy with God and glory to God.

Consider Job's before-and-after scenario and see if you find yourself more in one place than the other—and possibly in need of an extreme makeover.

Before this last chapter, Job was not surrendered; he did a lot of talking. Here are just a few instances of Job's intention to speak his mind to God. "I will not keep silent; I will speak out in the anguish of my spirit, I will complain in the bitterness of my soul" (Job 7:11). Do you notice all of the "I will's"? "I desire to speak to the Almighty and to argue my case with God" (Job 13:3). "If only I knew where to find him; if only I could go to his dwelling! I would state my case before him and fill my mouth with arguments. I would find out what he would answer me, and consider what he would say" (Job 23:3–5). My, my. Is it not somewhat brazen to state that he would consider what the Almighty would say?

When God started asking His own penetrating questions, Job's repentance began. He said, "I am unworthy—how can I reply to you? I put my hand over my mouth" (Job 40:4).

Finally!

Before Job's new realizations, he had only heard about God. He felt justified in standing up for his rights and his personal agenda. After his awakening, he repented. He yielded to God's touch. He took God's counsel and started listening. Before, he had God all figured out. After, he started bowing to the mystery. "Surely I spoke of things I did not understand, things too wonderful for me to know" (Job 42:3).

Before Job's surrender, he demanded answers to his own questions. He even had the audacity to put God on trial. In Job 7:20 he spat this question to the Almighty: "If I have sinned, what have I done to you, O watcher of men? Why have you made me your target? Have I become a burden to you?"

But as Job's heart softened under the humbling hand of his loving God, he was able to hear this question from the Most High: "Would you discredit my justice? Would you condemn me to justify yourself? Do you have an arm like God's, and can your voice thunder like his?" (Job 40:8–9).

As John White teaches in *Daring to Draw Near* (Inter-Varsity, 1977), before Job's surrender, he was big but puffed up. After God's probing questions about His creation, Job was small, but lifted up. Before, Job taught the majesty and glory of God. After, he treasured God's glory and worshiped Him. Before, Job was familiar with God. After, he was intimate with the Almighty.

Consider John White's further contrasts:

> We confuse intimacy with its counterfeit, familiarity. Intimacy is what we want but familiarity is all we achieve.
>
> Intimacy is dangerous, a knowing and a being known deeply and profoundly. Intimacy involves a true knowing. Familiarity is the illusion of knowing in which I see only what I want to see, only that part of a person that I can cope with. Intimacy involves a respectful listening and a respectful hearing.

At a glance, this is Job's journey:

Before	After
Unsurrendered	Surrendered
God all figured out	Bowing to the mystery
Speaking	Listening
Demanding answers to his questions	Humbly answering God's questions
Worldly sorrow	Godly sorrow
Familiar with God	Intimate with God
Instructing others in God's majesty	In awe of God's majesty
Ears that had heard of God	Eyes that have seen God
Standing up for personal rights	Repentance
Out-talking his friends	Putting a hand over his mouth
Big and puffed up	Small and lifted up

I long for it to be said of both you and me that "the LORD blessed the latter part of [our lives] more than the first" (Job 42:12). As Paul explains, spiritual growth is of God's doing: "I planted the seed, Apollos watered it, but God made it grow. So neither he who plants nor he who waters is anything, but only God, who makes things grow" (1 Corinthians 3:6–7). God longs for surrender in our journey toward intimacy; a heart already planted and watered, welcoming His touch.

What does it take for us to surrender to Him? Generally, broken and contrite hearts are what He specializes in reviving (see Isaiah 57:15). And further, humility—depending on Him—is what motivates His hand to lift us up (see 1 Peter 5:6). Just knowing information about Him is not what God longs for. He wants to touch our lives so that transformation and growth can occur. This is not just an intellectual feast where our minds dine on data. No, He wants our hearts to encounter Him. He longs for us to listen and bow to the mystery. He wants us to come to the great feast and sit under His banner of love.

God's Favorite Word

Are you beginning to see your name on the invitation? Our understanding of the width of God's love is not a matter of how much knowledge we have of God, but how much of us He has. Lasting spiritual growth comes not from knowing and doing more, but from surrendering to the Holy Spirit more. Every time we say yes to His banquet invitation, we yield, and that step toward Him is the beginning of surrender. We can stop being can-do people and bow before our can-do God. This is not about how wide our knowledge is or how vast our list of deeds, but about the width of His feast offering.

We need divine help to come near to Him. Jesus said, "No one can come to me unless the Father who sent me draws him" (John 6:44). But when we take even a baby step toward Him, He promises to gallop in our direction. "Come near to God and he will come near to you" (James 4:8). The rest of that verse says: "Wash your hands, you sinners, and purify your hearts, you double-minded."

Coming to Him is what defines growth in faith. Every time Jesus commended someone in the New Testament for showing faith, it was because he or she took a step toward Him. The following acrostic may help. Faith is:

> F —Feet
> A —Always
> I —Inclined
> T —Toward
> H —Him

I believe God's favorite word is *come* and He says it with arms open wide. Why do I think this is His favorite word? Because He says it passionately to so many different people. "Come to Me," He says to the weary (see Matthew 11:28–30). "Come near," He says to those removed (see James 4:8). "Come to Me and drink," He says to the thirsty (see John 7:37–39). "Come, follow Me," He says to those stumbling along in their own ruts (see Matthew 4:19–20). "Come out," He says to Lazarus and others who are experiencing death and stench in personal tombs (see John 11:43). "Come, let us reason together," He says to transgressors with scarlet sins (see Isaiah 1:18).

"Come up here," He summons those gazing upon His throne (see Revelation 4:1–2). "Come, you who have a case against Me," He says to those angry with Him (see Isaiah 50:8, NASB). "Come and have breakfast," He says to the hungry (see John 21:12). "Come listen," He says to those yearning to grow in the fear of the Lord (see Psalm 34:11). "Come down immediately," He says to Zacchaeus and others dreaming of redemption and transformation (see Luke 19:5). "Come with Me," He says to His beloved (see Song of Songs 2:10).

Surely you can find yourself somewhere in that stack of invitations. And with every answer of yes comes a reward. If you are weary, you can find rest. If you are a distance away, you get to come closer. If you are thirsty, you can drink. If you are doing your own thing, you can start following His way. If there is death anywhere in your spirit or soul, you can answer His call to choose life. If sin has you in a stronghold, you can accept His offer of rescue and freedom.

If you "come up," new revelation is yours. If you are angry with Him, you can come face-to-face with the loving God. If you are hungry, He will feed you. If you want knowledge of the fear of the Lord, you can come and listen. If you are willing to climb down from any high place you have made for yourself, you can know transformation and restoration in your life.

You see, He is not looking for a corporate executive in a business or a brilliant scientist in an experimental lab or an event coordinator for a family reunion, although that is how some evangelical churches today are operating. He does not need a star for an entertainment venue or a caretaker for an institution or even a wedding planner. No, He is looking for a bride who will come to the wedding feast with Him. The spiritual growth that leads to that place of intimacy only happens with surrender.

To find rest at the feast, you must take His yoke—not yours or anyone else's. You have to "leave your nets" to follow Him, surrendering the familiar. You need to yield to life, not what draws toward death. It requires reasoning together, not leaning on your own understanding (see Proverbs 3:5–6). You must surrender inferior refreshments to enjoy the living water and the bread of life. You must stop speaking if you are to listen. You must, like Zacchaeus, forsake the impossible task of pleasing men in order to please God. He wants you to come to Him. He wants to lock eyes with you. He wants you to enjoy the feast prepared for you.

Come to the feast and remain in His banquet hall. Mystery and intimacy are waiting. Come. Linger. Allow Him to convince you that His banner over you is love.

Searching for More

1. Share about the most lavish banquet you have ever attended. How did it compare with God's feast?
2. Reread Job 42:1–6 and review the evidence given in this chapter of Job before and after his surrendered

response to God. Which column defines you most? What personal strengths and weaknesses do you recognize in yourself?

3. Which of the "Come" invitations most draws your attention? Why? (See Appendix 1.)

_____ To the weary
_____ To those far away
_____ To the thirsty
_____ To those doing their own thing
_____ To those at a place of death
_____ To sinners
_____ To those wanting a new revelation
_____ To those angry with God
_____ To the hungry
_____ To those with cotton in their ears
_____ To those longing for transformation
_____ To the beloved

2

Taste and See

A group of about forty adults from our church's praise team were sitting in our basement watching a video teaching from Louie Giglio. Louie leads a ministry known as Passion, reaching out to college kids who long to grow in every dimension so they can give God glory for His name and renown.

As Louie's words unfolded, I got it. He started talking about doughnuts of all things. In fact the title of the message was "The Gospel According to Krispy Kreme." He told his audience, live and on video, many facts about the company—such as where the headquarters is located and how the neon Hot sign comes on at franchises to announce when the freshest of the fresh are ready. We learned that if you are really in the know you do not call the product "Krispy Kremes"; you merely call them "Kremes." We were also privy to the company's policy on quality control. We all laughed as Louie straightened himself up and said proudly,

"I've memorized the whole thing." Here was a man who knew his subject!

As the dissertation continued, my eyes were drawn to a box of Krispy Kremes sitting center stage. It actually seemed to be steaming. It had Louie's attention, too. He glanced frequently in the carton's direction with longing. At one point he took a step closer. Finally, with a somewhat desperate voice, he said, "Would you mind if I just took one little bite?"

The audience seated before him—and the group in our basement—seemed to be perplexed. This was quite irregular. Eating a doughnut in the middle of a discourse about our holy God? We all watched in wonder as Louie took several minutes to enjoy the doughnut, complete with *oohs*, *aahs* and licking sounds. Before he was finished, icing was smeared all over his fingers and mouth.

The facts about Krispy Kremes were one thing. Interesting. Impressive even. But watching him bite into that warm, crème-filled, chocolate-glazed creation was quite another. By the time he was finished, all I wanted was a doughnut. And I wanted all the people around me to savor the doughnuts, too.

Of course, Louie was not trying to sell doughnuts. He was helping us respond to God's invitation in Psalm 34:8: "Taste and see that the LORD is good." The facts are not bad. We just need to use them to move toward God. In like manner, people who are interested in moving beyond facts and into an intimate relationship savor their God. No, they *s-a-a-a-a-a-a-vor* Him. And that spells growth.

This taste-and-see experience is irreplaceable. It is what the feast is all about. People who are growing bow to the wonder. And then their delight in the God of the faith replaces their duty in the disciplines of the faith. They still read their

Bibles—but now rather than put a checkmark beside that completed chore on their to-do lists, they meet God there. They continue praying—but now rather than offer a lengthy monologue of demands, they share in a dialogue. They still tithe—but now rather than labor over instructions about biblical percentages, they respond to the heartbeat of God. David Jeremiah, in *My Heart's Desire* (Integrity, 2002), captures the essence of this taste-and-see phenomenon. He says:

> It's possible to focus so intensely on gaining knowledge *about* God that we miss the knowledge *of* God. The difference there is one of eternal, infinite magnitude. It's the difference between seeing an old, faded picture of a distant relative and sitting in your granddaddy's lap. It's the difference between reading a scientific, statistical report about the vitamins in beef and biting into a thick sirloin steak hot off the grill. It's the difference between knowing facts about God and experiencing His powerful presence. I believe that as a whole, we modern evangelical Christians are far guiltier of dry intellectual faith than we ever want to realize. Ultimately it feels so much safer to limit ourselves to sharing information about the Lord.

Have you accepted His invitation but still hesitate to take a chair at the great feast? Would you dare to admit that you are not sure of God's love for you all the time? Allow me to share with you how He convinced me to taste and see.

Love That Pursues

The high school gym was decorated for our student talent show and the audience was full of smiling faces. But I was nervous. "I can't believe we're doing this," I said to my friend who had agreed to do a dance routine with me. Then I added, "Did you see that guy with the dark curly hair? He's playing trumpet in the band. I think he's going to ask me out." Giggles enveloped us.

Later that evening, the curly-haired guy's dad—who had been at the high school to support his son in the band—said, "I think you should ask that little blonde out on a date." The boy blurted, "I already did." John had chosen me and so had his father.

I knew John desired me; granted, his moves were not very smooth. (We were only fifteen.) In the movie theater there would be the inevitable yawn with arms stretched outward. The arm closest to me always seemed to find a resting place around my shoulders. And when we walked alongside each other he consistently reached for my hand to hold, sometimes swinging it with carefree ease.

"Is John calling again?" my mother would ask. "You just saw him an hour ago." The phone calls multiplied because it seemed he thought of me often. Then gifts arrived. Flowers. Candy. Tickets to someplace special. One time he took me on a bus tour to Ravinia Park near Chicago for a classical concert. Our excitement waned when we realized that we were the only teenagers on a whole busload of senior citizens.

He sent love letters. As he toured the country over the summers with a concert band, he found many opportunities to write sweet notes of endearment. Not once did I set an offering aside to be read at a later time. No, I waited for the postman, pulled the letter out of his hand, tore it open, read it, reread it and reread it again. I stuffed it under my pillow with a flashlight so I could read it after curfew. I wondered, "What did he mean by that?" I read between the lines. And I saved everything.

Then I began practicing his name. You know. I wrote on endless pieces of notepaper, "John R. Anderes, Jr." "John and Marilyn Anderes." "Mr. and Mrs. John R. Anderes, Jr." "Marilyn Anderes." "Mrs. John Anderes." Over and over. His name was important to me.

We daydreamed together and carved our initials on trees. I could today find a special tree in the middle of Wisconsin's Kettle Moraine State Forest that holds our initials, but probably in a different shape and texture by now.

We cuddled. We fit just right. We are still good at cuddling, although the configurations have changed some. We kissed. And we started making plans for commitment.

Then one day in August 1965, six years after we started dating, I stood in a white veil and gown and he in a black tuxedo before a God we did not yet know personally and said, "You are mine," "I will" and "I do."

Intimacy came, physically and spiritually. Since that time there have been many smiles and countless tears. We have skipped into "date days" and sweated side by side over garden planting and harvesting, garage cleanings and toy gatherings. We have thrown our heads back in uncontrolled laughter, and we have wept together at births, deaths, revelations, gratefulness and the challenges of rearing three children.

Sacrifices were made, one for the other. And through it all, faithfulness.

Why do I tell you this? Because joyful earthly love is a reflection of God's dynamic, passionate, pursuing love. God's love and wooing is also a courtship. The truth is this: God is your Lover. God is my Lover.

Human love is never a perfect analogy for God's love simply because we are all flawed individuals. Even with the storybook start that John and I had, there were times that our humanness threatened to destroy what God had brought together. It was, in fact, through a particularly difficult time that the Holy Spirit poured out the Father's love into my heart in a wonderful way—though not a way I would have chosen.

John and I were suffering through a period of discontent with many things, especially each other. Twenty-six years of marriage had not brought us any closer to understanding the depths of each other's hearts. One evening we had a knock-down, drag-out fight. Unfair, angry words spewed everywhere. I had had it. So I, a grown woman, got in the car and ran away.

I drove around the community for two hours and, getting tired of that, decided to see if our friends, the Bradys, would take me in. I found that they were out of town, so I thought I would go to our pastor and his wife. I knew, however, that they would send me home with their prayers so we could work it out. So after driving another hour, I realized that I had nowhere to go . . . but home. I thought, *I'll go home, but I will not speak to him.*

The porch light was on as I turned into the driveway and I saw John standing in the doorframe. I got out of the car and stepped onto the porch. *Keep your resolve, Marilyn,* I told myself. *Don't speak.* But that decision melted away because I saw that my husband was waiting for me with his arms of love open wide. It was an embrace I could not resist. Then, when I finally stumbled into the house and melted in his arms in the vestibule, my heart reeling with many emotions, he shared something profound.

"I've been praying, Marilyn, and I think God has already answered. There is no doubt that we love each other, but we seem to have a hard time showing it." He looked at me with tender courage and continued. "I think it's because we don't truly believe that God loves us." He paused a moment to let that sink in. "So it seems we need to start asking Him to show us how much He loves us."

John and I had been saved for twenty years, yet God's love was still an idea in our heads and a message on our lips, not a truth in our hearts. We had no idea how to taste and see His goodness. Not really. So we began to ask God to show us how much He loves us, and He heard our prayers. He showed His love to us magnificently. And in the succeeding years God convinced both my husband and me that He is the passionate, wild lover of our souls.

Perhaps your story of human love is something like mine. Or maybe you see only the shattered shards of dreams. Perhaps your love story is nonexistent or stale and you feel anything but pursued. Perhaps you think that the great feast is going to be just one more big disappointment. But do you know that where human love fails, a greater, wider embrace of Love waits for you? Do you know that the Love above all loves desires you passionately—and is at this moment pursuing, courting you, bidding you to taste and see His goodness? Consider the evidence of His holy passion for you.

- *He chooses us.* "Long before he laid down earth's foundations, he had us in mind, had settled on us as the focus of his love, to be made whole and holy by his love. . . . (What pleasure he took in planning this!)" (Ephesians 1:4–5, MESSAGE). The Son chooses us and so does the Father.
- *He desires us.* "I carried you on eagles' wings and brought you to myself. . . . You will be my treasured possession" (Exodus 19:4–5).
- *He thinks about us.* "How precious [concerning me] are your thoughts, O God! How vast is the sum of them!" (more literal translation of Psalm 139:17).

- *He pursues us.* "You will be called Sought After" (Isaiah 62:12).

- *He gives us gifts.* "He who did not spare his own Son, but gave him up for us all—how will he not also, along with him, graciously give us all things?" (Romans 8:32).

- *He sends us love letters.* "I will put my laws in their minds and write them on their hearts" (Hebrews 8:10). And I dare not put off reading His love letter—the Bible—until it is more convenient or comfortable for my schedule. No, I want to read it, reread it and read between the lines. I want to read it afterhours and savor the lines just for me. I want Psalm 138:2 to be true of me: "You [God] have exalted above all things your name and your word."

- *He cuddles with us.* "He gathers the lambs in his arms and carries them close to his heart" (Isaiah 40:11). That sounds like cuddling to me!

- *He carves our initials.* "See, I have engraved you on the palms of my hands" (Isaiah 49:16).

- *He makes a commitment to us.* "I gave you my solemn oath and entered into a covenant with you, declares the Sovereign Lord, and you became mine" (Ezekiel 16:8).

- *He sacrifices for us.* "But God demonstrates his own love for us in this: While we were still sinners, Christ died for us" (Romans 5:8).

- *He is intimate with us.* "The Lord confides in those who fear him" (Psalm 25:14). Doesn't it thrill you to know you are God's confidante? Song of Songs 6:3 says: "I am my lover's and my lover is mine."

- *He is faithful to us.* "Know therefore that the Lord your God is God; he is the faithful God, keeping his covenant of love to a thousand generations of those who love him and keep his commands" (Deuteronomy 7:9).

- And *He sings love songs to us.* "The LORD . . . will take great delight in you . . . he will rejoice over you with singing" (Zephaniah 3:17). The word *delight* means twirling with intensity.

When I realized that God does all of that and more, I began to desire Him. It was the beginning of my heart knowledge of the intimacy of God's love. I began to want more than anything to come to His table.

The Bible gives us a beautiful rendering of that heart response. It is found in the words of Jesus' mother, Mary, a young woman who came joyfully to the feast and accepted all that was prepared for her. Let's look at the familiar story—familiar, that is, to our own awakening hearts as we draw nearer to His table.

God's Embrace

Mary loved God because He loved her first. And the love she was convinced of caused her to utter incredible things to the lover of her soul.

Look at the beautiful words of the Magnificat:

"My soul glorifies the Lord and my spirit rejoices in God my Savior, for he has been mindful of the humble state of his servant. From now on all generations will call me blessed, for the Mighty One has done great things for me—holy is his name. His mercy extends to those who fear him, from generation to generation. He has performed mighty deeds with his arm; he has scattered those who are proud in their inmost thoughts. He has brought down rulers from their thrones but has lifted up the humble. He has filled the hungry with good things but has sent the rich away empty. He has helped his servant Israel, remembering to be merciful to Abraham and his descendants forever, even as he said to our fathers."

Luke 1:46–55

How did Mary know God loved her? The evidence is plentiful. First, God sent an angel to bring a proclamation. Luke 1:28 resounds: "Greetings, you who are highly favored! The Lord is with you." Then He recognized her fear and continued His personal message to lay aside her concerns. "Do not be afraid, Mary, you have found favor with God" (Luke 1:30). She would give birth to a child, One who would be great and would be called the Son of the Most High, with a kingdom that never ends (see Luke 1:32–33).

God poured out His love still more by answering Mary's deepest question about the birth of this child promised to her; a query born not of unbelief but of a genuine desire to know. "How will this be . . . since I am a virgin?" (Luke 1:34). This was her child and she knew she had never been with a man. You can bet we all would have had some questions. But the angel answered, "The Holy Spirit will come upon you, and the power of the Most High will overshadow you" (Luke 1:35).

And to convince Mary even more of His passionate love for her, God sent help her way. Elizabeth was an older, respected relative with a due date six months ahead of the virgin. She could help guide Mary. The angel declared: "She who was said to be barren is in her sixth month. For nothing is impossible with God" (Luke 1:36–37). That statement alone would have put some of Mary's concerns to rest. No wonder she was able to voice her love so freely and eloquently.

God's love beckons us to draw near. In *The Pressure's Off* (Waterbrook, 2002), Larry Crabb says we can be "known in loving safety, explored with genuine interest, discovered by hopeful wisdom, and touched from the source of spiritual power." And when we know we are loved, we can accept God's plan for our lives, even if it does not make sense to us. Mary made yet another incredible statement: "I am the Lord's servant. . . . May it be to me as you have said" (Luke 1:38).

There will be only one virgin birth. God dealt with Mary in ways unique to her, but some of it is applicable to our own yearnings. The salutation that the angel brought is for us all: "Greetings, you who are highly favored! The Lord is with you." Do you believe it? Even a scant reading of God's Word confirms that truth. You are favored. He is with you. What is more, He meets you at your point of fear. It has been said that God's admonition "Do not fear" is listed no less than 365 times in the Bible. That is one for each day of the year. He answers your deepest questions. He helps you know that nothing is impossible with Him. He sends help alongside. And you can understand that you are His servant and can be content for all to be "as He has said" in your life.

How is that possible? "The Holy Spirit will come upon you, and the power of the Most High will overshadow you." The Convincer is at work all the time. Romans 5:5 bears repeating: "God has poured out his love into our hearts by the Holy Spirit, whom he has given us."

Because of this you can adore God as Mary did. You can join others at the feast and say, "My soul glorifies the Lord

and my spirit rejoices in God my Savior. The Mighty One
has done great things for me—holy is his name."

It makes no difference what season of life you are in. The
greeting is the same. You are highly favored. The Lord is
with you. Consider God's Word to you in Ecclesiastes 3:1–8.
Ask God to help you decide where you might be right now.
And remember His greeting.

> There is a time for everything, and a season for every
> activity under heaven: a time to be born and a time
> to die, a time to plant and a time to uproot, [You are
> highly favored. The Lord is with you.]
> a time to kill and a time to heal, a time to tear down and
> a time to build, [You are highly favored. The Lord is
> with you.]
> a time to weep and a time to laugh, a time to mourn and
> a time to dance, [You are highly favored. The Lord is
> with you.]
> a time to scatter stones and a time to gather them, a time
> to embrace and a time to refrain, [You are highly fa-
> vored. The Lord is with you.]
> a time to search and a time to give up, a time to keep and
> a time to throw away, [You are highly favored. The
> Lord is with you.]
> a time to tear and a time to mend, a time to be silent and
> a time to speak, [You are highly favored. The Lord is
> with you.]
> a time to love and a time to hate, a time for war and a
> time for peace. [You are highly favored. The Lord is
> with you.]

Luke's account of Mary in the Christmas story brings
season's greetings to you and me: No matter what the
season, the greeting is the same. Mary loved because He
first loved her. I love because He first loved me. You can

love Him intimately because He first loves you. Love begets love.

Are you convinced? Like Mary, do you believe God's greeting? You are highly favored. He is with you. Are you persuaded that He notices your fears, answers your deepest questions and helps you know that "nothing is impossible" with Him? Has the Holy Spirit come upon you? Are you aware of the power of the Most High convincing you of His passionate love for you? If you are not, you can ask Him for help. It is that simple.

You are chosen, desired, thought about, pursued, given gifts, sent love letters, and cuddled. He has carved your initials on the palms of His hands. He is in covenant with you and He has sacrificed His all for you. He is the faithful God who sings His beautiful love song over you, His beloved. And, He longs for intimacy. He wants to embrace you at the banquet table.

Will you taste and see?

Searching for More

1. The lover of our souls breathes His Word into our hearts, convincing us of His passion. Which of these verses touches you the most and why? (See Appendix 2.)

    _____ He chooses us (see Ephesians 1:4–5).
    _____ He desires us (see Exodus 19:4–5).
    _____ He thinks about us (see Psalm 139:17).
    _____ He pursues us (see Isaiah 62:12).
    _____ He gives us gifts (see Romans 8:32).
    _____ He sends us love letters (see Hebrews 8:10).
    _____ He cuddles with us (see Isaiah 40:11).

_____ He carves our initials (see Isaiah 49:16).

_____ He makes a commitment to us (see
Ezekiel 16:8).

_____ He sacrifices for us (see Romans 5:8).

_____ He is intimate with us (see Psalm 25:14;
Song of Songs 6:3).

_____ He is faithful to us (see Deuteronomy
7:9).

_____ He sings love songs to us (see Zephaniah
3:17).

2. How do you know that you are highly favored by God?
What evidence do you have that He cares about your
fears and answers your deepest questions?
3. Has the Holy Spirit come upon you? How are you
aware of the power of the Most High overshadowing
you to convince you of His love?

3

We Had to Celebrate

You can tell a lot about people by the hugs they give or do not give. Some are stiff and uncomfortable. Some inappropriate. Some are an obvious duty and some keep you in their control. But some are warm and giving and you feel safe, strengthened, revitalized and . . . at home.

God longs for us to be at home in His embrace. He wants us to dance at His banquet celebration and come alive to His love. But sometimes even if we are convinced of His love we still feel unworthy. The Word is careful to declare that God wants us close. In Jeremiah 30:21, God asks this penetrating question: "Who is he [or she] who will devote himself [or herself] to be close to me?" Psalm 34:18 states that "the LORD is close to the brokenhearted." Ephesians 2:13 says: "Now in Christ Jesus you who once were far away have been brought near through the blood of Christ." Brought near.

wider

Arms of Welcome

One day at Dulles airport in Northern Virginia I got a human picture of His embrace, the kind we receive when we enter His banquet hall and come to His table.

Our daughter and her husband were to return home from a European trek and it was my privilege to bring their two children, Hannah, eight, and Kyle, five, to meet them at the airport. I knew that the trip around the Washington, D.C., beltway would take at least an hour, so I made a "WELCOME HOME" poster for the kids to decorate and color on the way. And I picked up a bouquet of roses for Kyle to give his mom.

The children were kept busy during the ride, creating a masterpiece for their parents, and before long we trundled our way into the terminal. Hannah oversaw the poster, and Kyle dusted the floor with his upside-down bouquet. Smiles and pointing fingers followed us all along our path to the gate.

When we finally arrived at our destination, I saw a large area cordoned off for the passengers who were deplaning. Not only did heavy cords frame the forbidden area, but a bold sign on our side read Do Not Cross This Line. Our wait became somewhat tedious. Hannah sat cross-legged and Kyle lay on the floor with the roses covering his head.

Finally the door swung open and the children sprang into alertness. They waited. And they waited some more. Before too long, their mom and dad came through the door. Neither Hannah nor Kyle cared one bit that the sign said Do Not Cross. All they wanted to do was to crush in close to their parents. What ensued was precious. Dad's big arms were around everyone. Mom cried. And the children chattered incessant questions and comments. It was a happy reunion.

No one felt unworthy to be in the arms of the other. No one minded the officious sign forbidding contact. And everyone watching smiled with delight.

That is what it is like when we fall into the arms of our Beloved. We anticipate the reunion and snuggle into His embrace with ease and a certain "comfortableness" we know nowhere else. What a glad gathering!

Jesus' story of the Prodigal Son, told in Luke 15:11–32, shows how a fraudulent, flawed life has hope for a full-face, open-armed encounter with the God of the feast. Perhaps you, too, have felt unworthy, undeserving of the hug He offers. But, my friend, you and I are no more—or less—flawed than this ungrateful son of the father. God does not see our blemishes. He sees our hearts and longs for them to be as His is. Let's take a look at this story.

The Six "Ds" of the Prodigal's Journey

Six words describe the journey of this wayward son. Before we go into this pilgrimage, I repeat that not one of us is exempt from wayward thinking and behaving. We are all sinners with a heart that is prone to wander. So, the trek of this bad boy may well be your journey; it is most certainly mine. The six phases of his life adventure are Deception, Deliverance, Decision, Discovery, Displeasure and Dance. My prayer is that by the time we consider them, you will no longer feel unworthy to twirl at God's party. You will run into His arms.

1. Deception

The text says that the Prodigal "set off for a distant country" (Luke 15:13). It seems he thought that any place away from his father was preferred to being close. He was a self-ish lad with a self-serving mantra: "What's mine is mine and what's yours is mine." In those days, no one received an inheritance without the death of a loved one occurring first, so by asking for his money early, the Prodigal was essentially saying, "I wish you were dead."

Now we would never voice such a thing to our heavenly Father. But actions speak louder than words. How often do we cling to things that hinder us from full devotion to Jesus?

Picture this in your mind: Suppose you are standing in a room that is filled with small items on the floor, each one representing a different aspect of your daily life. Pretend to pick up items as the story unfolds and realize that once one is picked up, you cannot put it back down.

For the sake of this illustration, imagine that you have just been named employee of the year for your successful urban design. Pick up that plastic city map. You are asked to travel to other communities and share your ideas. Pick up that model airplane. You will need some new clothes—represented by that small clothing bag.

And on it goes. With the increase in pay, you decide to do some decorating around your home, to buy a new car, to have a party for your friends—and into your arms go the lamp, toy car, party hat. The load is getting harder to manage.

Then you realize you have been neglecting your church responsibilities and your Bible study group—but it is almost impossible to pick up the women's ministry dinner decorations and the big Bible. Finally, you realize that you have lost sight of the picture of Jesus that was once so precious to you. But to find it among all the "things" around you and hold it high means that you have to let go of everything else.

Do you get the point? None of those things is bad. Not unless it gets in the way of being near Jesus and following His command to carry His name before a needy world. Clothes and cars and church duties and success are not a problem, but they can get in the way of being close to God. Good things are not always best things. Sometimes the good stuff propels us to the distant country and the transition is so subtle we do not even know it is happening. We become deceived.

Then, too, we are sometimes guilty of being on the other side of the coin. Eager for others to be successful, we suggest new ways for them to carry all the stuff that is actually keeping them from being close to the Father's side at the feast. Awareness is the first step to lasting help.

2. Deliverance

God tells us that the Prodigal "came to his senses" (Luke 15:17). "He began to be in need" (Luke 15:14) and knew that he could not fix his own situation. He started to experience a "go-through" that would usher him into a breakthrough; a deliverance of sorts.

In her work *Aurora Leigh*, Elizabeth Barrett Browning notes that "Earth's crammed with heaven, and every common bush afire with God. But only he who sees, takes off his shoes. The rest sit round it and pluck blackberries." Moses' experience at the burning bush apparently had an impact on her.

I recently went blackberry picking with our grandchildren at a nearby orchard. The fruit we gathered was sweet to the taste, beautiful to the eye, readily available and self-satisfying in the effort expended, not to mention a whole lot of fun. The berries were so large that they made a big noise as they went

51

into the bucket. They stained our fingers and the evidence of stolen nibbles was all over our mouths.

I cannot say what your spiritual blackberries—things that keep you perpetually plucking at the bush—look like. They are different for all of us. But I am beginning to understand what mine look like. I am coming to my senses. They are sweet and big, readily available and appealing to my fleshly side. They make a big prideful noise in the gathering and they are often lots of fun. They leave stains. And they are deadly, because they keep me from seeing the fire in the bush and taking off my shoes before God's holiness.

My spiritual blackberries are things like being concerned with reputation over repentance. Dignity and honor over deliverance. Human programs over God's presence. Doing instead of being. They are formulas over fresh revelation. Information over transformation. Answers and activity instead of adoration. They are inhibition instead of being inhabited by the living God. Spiritual bulliness instead of brokenness. Intellect without intimacy. They are "God-all-figured-out" instead of a heart bowing to the mystery. Endless committee meetings instead of watching after people's souls. They are homiletics instead of humility. They are "spin" instead of surrender.

Like the Prodigal, we need to come to our senses. We need to ponder the longings of God's heart. We need to desire His embrace. We need deliverance from anything that blots out true intimacy.

3. Decision

"I will set out and go back to my father" (Luke 15:18).

It was the pronouncement of a choice made in the heart. It was the indication of a person being humbled. God is clear about His desire in this regard. First Peter 5:5–6 peals:

"'God opposes the proud but gives grace to the humble.' Humble yourselves, therefore, under God's mighty hand, that he may lift you up in due time." I made such a determination. God humbled me when He flashed a picture of myself before my eyes.

My husband and I were vacationing with friends at Lone Peak near Bozeman, Montana. We sat on a porch enjoying the mountain view and marveling at the wild flowers. But our eyes were suddenly jerked away from that colorful array by the furious flapping of wings. We looked up to see two very different sights. One was the flock of little flitting birds that had caught our attention. The other was just beyond them—a majestic soaring eagle. The acrobatics of both kinds of birds spurred wonder in our hearts, and we could not help noticing the difference between the little birds' flapping and the great eagle's sailing.

The tiny ones seemed driven, using all the energy they could muster just to keep themselves propelled. The eagle, however, seemed to drift effortlessly on currents of air. I imagined that if I could get close enough, I would probably hear the flitting ones gasping for their next breaths in the thin air, while all was easy for the eagle.

It seemed the small birds shot furtive glances in our direction; I could imagine they were worried about our watching them. The eagle, on the other hand, seemed hardly to give us a thought. We were nonthreatening humans sitting on a lesser perch.

For several months I pondered the contrast of flapping and soaring, and I decided it was a perfect picture of what God had been helping me to understand. And it prompted a life-altering decision.

When the year 2000 arrived, I greeted the new millennium having known Jesus as many years as I had not known

Him. The first 28 years of my life I paid no attention to Him. I went to Sunday school because all little girls from polite families in the 1950s did that. I went to youth group. I sang in the choir. I played the piano at the nursing home. I knew a lot about Jesus but I did not know Jesus.

The second 28 years of my life started in January 1972, when God revealed Himself to me. I understood that Jesus' sacrifice on the cross bridged the gap my sin had created between me and the Father. It was not a burning-bush time, but He did light up my kitchen, and I knelt on the tile floor and prayed an unsophisticated prayer: "I don't know who You are or all that You want, but I think You want me. So, okay." I am grateful for many people who poured their own knowing into my heart, and I began the journey of "more of Him and less of me."

During that second set of 28 years, I did a lot of flapping. I was intense about my walk with Jesus. I never missed a quiet time. I read my Bible every day and prayed the required ten minutes every morning. I memorized Scripture, even whole books. I made sure that my stack of memory-verse cards was noticeably higher than anyone else's. I went to seminars. I gave testimonies at movie theaters and went on door-to-door neighborhood campaigns. I was part of many small groups and taught Bible studies. I led women's retreats from Wyoming to Florida. But feasting with God was a mystery to me. I was too busy. It was an intellectual understanding without the intimacy. There was rejoicing over how God met the longings of my heart, but no thought that He might have longings for my heart.

The pace accelerated and I kept up. I hosted missionary families and provided temporary shelter for those needing a bed or a family. I did everything I could think to do. But my days were becoming lifeless. I was exhausted and my spirit felt dull. There had to be more than this.

You may have noticed the numbers of "I's" "me's" and "my's" in that last paragraph. That is because the flapping was all about me. But God seemed excited, or at least persistent, to help a 28-year-old spiritual child in a 56-year-old body learn to soar. He seemed to want to connect with me. He longed for me to know His passionate love. I learned that all the disciplines are good and right and necessary for spiritual growth. After all, "faith by itself, if it is not accompanied by action, is dead" (James 2:17). But devoid of passion for God—sitting at the table feasting with Him—all those deeds added up to a tired body and a resentful spirit. So I made a choice. I opted not just to say He had first place, but to make Him my number one priority.

Perhaps you, too, have been doing all the "right" things. Maybe you, too, have been stacking verse cards and keeping tallies of good deeds, trying desperately to be worthy of the attention He is giving you at the banquet. Perhaps you have felt something stirring, a need inside of you, something that you cannot articulate. It is a feeling that will not go away. Maybe you are homesick for the Father's embrace, but you do not know how to run to His arms and gaze into His eyes.

Do you want to exchange all your exhausting activity for feasting with Him? Do you long to enjoy the rich fare God intended for you? Do you want to stop flapping and start soaring amidst the peaks? Do you want to trade plodding for dancing? Do you want to go beyond a personal relationship with God to an intimate love affair with Him? Only one person wants this even more than you, and that is God. Let this be the day you make the decision to receive His embrace.

4. Discovery

The account says that the father "ran to his son" (Luke 15:20). What an eye-opener! I suspect the Prodigal did not know what to expect, but I imagine that he was prone to think the father would wag a finger in his face and make him promise to do better next time. Instead . . . this respected head of the household ran eagerly to meet him.

The Father, our Father, is rarely as we expect Him to be.

I met a woman named Michelle at a Christian retreat that I led and was amazed to watch her story unfold. Actually, she almost did not attend the retreat because of a crushing personal circumstance. Just a week prior, she had miscarried a baby, a child that she ached for. She was obviously broken over this loss of life but decided to come anyway. She opted to come to the feast to meet God, not stay away from Him.

The weekend found her interested but unmoved. She told me that she was not sure why God had been so strong in His prompting for her to come. On Sunday morning she knew why. As the worship service began, the leader invited each woman attending to write a prayer request on a 3 x 5 card. Michelle showed me what she had written. With tearstains evident, the prayer card revealed her longing to kiss her now deceased baby: *Kiss him for me*, she pleaded.

The teaching for the morning was on the Prodigal Son. A young woman had been assigned to read the account from Luke 15. When she got to the twentieth verse she got confused and read the same words twice. With nervous giggles, she said, "Well, I guess someone really needed to hear that verse again." Luke 15:20 says this: "While he was still a long way off, his father saw him and was filled with compassion for him; he ran to his son, threw his arms around him and kissed him."

Michelle gasped. She knew that the Father had kissed her baby. Tears flowed. She had been the one who needed to hear that verse twice. She went to the altar to offer her thanks. A friend who did not know what she had written on her card prayed this over her: "Comfort Michelle, God. Kiss her now."

That young woman could have stayed away from the Father and never discovered His longing for her to feast with Him. She was hurt and fearful of being embarrassed by involuntary tears. But instead, she came to the retreat at His bidding. She exercised faith. She ran toward Him, and, as she did, He met her with a kiss for her baby and for her. And His love healed her heart. What a discovery!

5. Displeasure

Whenever anyone is getting close to understanding the feast God has prepared for her, there will always be those with raised eyebrows and foreboding frowns. This tale relates that the Prodigal's older brother "became angry and refused to go in" (Luke 15:28). I will have more to say about this religious spirit of displeasure in the next chapter.

6. Dance

The father planned. The father cavorted. The father gave. The father lavished.

"We had to celebrate," he declared (Luke 15:32). Our God is a celebration God. He wants to dance with us. Do you think there is no party in this life? Are you too busy? Are you afraid you don't know how to dance? Are you sure you are a wallflower?

There are many who try to convince us—like ugly stepsisters—that the ball is not for the likes of us. There is no feast. We are unlovely. Our ball gowns are tattered. Our feet are too big for the glass slipper. We do not belong at such an extravagant banquet. We have too many chores remaining. We are unworthy.

These are all lies. God is the lover of your soul, and He is longing for you to twirl with Him at His banquet. If you do not know how to dance, just stand on His feet and let Him whisk you along. Before long you will be dancing just like Him. There is a feast, a great banquet. See how wide and welcoming the table is! And you are the beloved. Jesus' righteousness makes you worthy to join in. Enthusiastic dancing is the appropriate thing for you to do at God's banquet. So kick up your heels. Enjoy Him.

Searching for More

1. In which position below do you find yourself at present? Explain your answer.

_____ Feeling that any place away from God is better than being near Him

_____ Coming to your senses; experiencing a "go-through" before the "breakthrough"

_____ Making your decision to go back to the Father

_____ Making the discovery that God is more interested in having you in His arms than He is in wagging His finger in your face

_____ Experiencing the displeasure of those who do not understand your desire to feast with God

_____ Dancing with abandon at God's banquet

2. What are your thoughts after reading the following quote? "A musician was playing on a very beautiful instrument, and the music so enraptured the people that they were driven to dance ecstatically. Then a deaf man who knew nothing of music passed by, and seeing the enthusiastic dancing of the people decided they must be insane" (The Baal Shem, quoted by Abraham Heschel, "God in Search of Man: A Philosophy of Judaism," in Ken Gire, *The Divine Embrace* [Wheaton: Tyndale, 2003], 166).

3. Do you hear the music? If you do, what is your plan for inviting others to the dance?

longer

The Marathon

Therefore, since we are surrounded by such a great cloud of witnesses, let us throw off everything that hinders and the sin that so easily entangles, and let us run with perseverance the race marked out for us. Let us fix our eyes on Jesus, the author and perfecter of our faith.

Hebrews 12:1–2

4
Running Well

*I*t was an autumn morning, way too early for my liking. But I wanted to cheer on my friend Pat who was running a marathon. His wife, several friends and I made up the company of witnesses to encourage him to reach his goal.

Pat had trained hard for many months. On the big day he joined hundreds of others to wend their way through the byways of Baltimore, Maryland. He knew where the water stations would be and where we could pop out of the crowd with our applause. He had studied the terrain and knew where the steeper trails lay and the possible impediments he might encounter.

At approximately the eighteen-mile mark, Pat hit the wall. That is the place familiar to runners where they tell their bodies to "pull out"—that is, *Move!*—but get no response. At this point some people get nauseated. Some get leg cramps that can be relieved only by kneading their muscles. Some stop, never to return to the race. It is here—at the wall—that runners must be determined to keep their eyes on the goal. Pat continued through the pain and finished the race at a good speed for a first-time marathoner.

Twenty-six miles is a long way to run and, except for the few who are way ahead of the pack, the race is not so much a competition against others as it is against yourself and your best effort to date. Those who complete their objectives have a sense of great joy. They say that the pain is worth it.

Hebrews 12:1–2 talks about such a race. It says:

> Therefore, since we are surrounded by such a great cloud of witnesses, let us throw off everything that hinders and the sin that so easily entangles, and let us run with perseverance the race marked out for us. Let us fix our eyes on Jesus, the author and perfecter of our faith, who for the joy set before him endured the cross, scorning its shame, and sat down at the right hand of the throne of God.

This race and God's invitation to run it are the hallmarks of the next dimension of becoming intimate with Him. His love stretches as long as the marathon before you. My guess is that at the feast you became convinced of His love and believe that His sufficiency covers your concerns about unworthiness. But what about the stuff that gets in the way?

In this chapter we will learn, first, how to persevere. Then in the next two chapters we will discuss the ways Jesus helps us throw off everything that hinders as well as the sin that so easily entangles.

Some of the things that slow your progress in the marathon may actually be unknown to you. Others are disgustingly familiar. They bother you like unrelenting ants at a picnic; collections of small annoyances adding up to one big stumble. Still others are like the wall. You cannot seem to get past them no matter how hard you try. Yet God still says run.

In the National Gallery of Art in Washington, D.C., hangs a mid-sixteenth-century masterpiece by Jan van Hemessen titled "Arise, Take Up Thy Bed, and Walk." This work is extravagant with hope because the artist depicts the biblical account from Luke 5:17–26 of the paralytic and his mat at the point just after Jesus healed him. The man is centered on the landscape, carrying a voluminous bed pack on his back. In this painting it is the legs of the man that are so amazing. They are strong, capable and flexed. Just moments before, the muscles were atrophied, helpless, hopeless.

In this chapter we will learn a number of aspects about persevering in the race from this man's story. Surprising, isn't it? How can a paralytic run a race? Only with the help of a God who longs for him to come close. Only enabled by friends sent alongside by the faithful One. Only by addressing what had him on his mat.

As we begin, let's remember this: While it is imperative to be aware of our snares, we have a higher goal. It is far more important to see Jesus, be intimate with Him, live in His agenda and bring glory to His name.

Let's now consider five facts that help us persevere in the spiritual race as we move into the next dimension of intimacy.

1. We Need Encouragement to Run

The witnesses mentioned in the verses above from Hebrews 12 surround the runner, so there must be at least several of them. In the case of my friend Pat, there were half a dozen or so of us cheering him on at the Baltimore marathon. And for the paralytic there were four. I call them rope-holders. These were the guys who tried to take their friend on his mat into the house where Jesus was speaking but could not get in because of the crowd. Undaunted, they climbed to the roof, broke through the layer of tiles, dug an opening and used ropes to lower their friend to a spot right in front of Jesus (see Luke 5:19). If they had just desired to hear the Master's teaching, they would not have had to go to all that trouble, because the homes in that land were open and airy. They could have heard what was being said even though the crowd was large.

But they were longing for their friend to have personal contact with Jesus; to be touched, not physically necessarily, but in his spirit and soul. To accomplish that goal they displayed organizational skills, courage, a sense of humor, physical strength and good timing. They had the right equipment and they were desperate to get to Jesus.

Are you desperate to get to Jesus for a word, a touch? Don't answer too quickly because such people are often rejected by others. In his book *Messy Spirituality* (Zondervan, 2003), Michael Yaconelli writes:

> In Jesus' day, desperate people who tried to get to Jesus were surrounded by religious people who either ignored or rejected those who were seeking to have their hunger for God filled. Sadly, not much has changed over the years. Desperate people don't do well in churches. They don't fit, and they don't cooperate in the furthering of their starvation. "Church people" often label "desperate people" as strange and unbalanced. But when desperate people get a taste of God, they can't stay away from Him, no matter what everyone around them thinks.

These four rope-holders were so desperate that they broke through politeness. They made a mess, but they accomplished their goal. The power of Jesus was there to heal the sick (see Luke 5:17). They had a sick friend. They were going to get him to Jesus no matter what.

The rope-holders in my life are people who have prayed for my husband and me to understand God's desire for a relationship with us. They are people who have cared for me and taught me the truths of Scripture. They are people who have stepped up to the plate on my behalf. Accountability partners. Mentors. Disciplers. Intercessors. Shield bearers. They are people who dared to come close to me so that I could come close to God. Do you have rope-holders in your life? And, further, are you a rope-holder for anyone else?

Our witnesses in this race need to know us and the goal we seek. They need to understand how important it is to finish the race. They run ahead of us at times, alongside us at others and sometimes even carry us close to the finish line so we can crawl over it if need be.

Paul offers valuable testimony in this regard. Acts 20:24 says: "I consider my life worth nothing to me, if only I may finish the race and complete the task the Lord Jesus has given me—the task of testifying to the gospel of God's grace." Then in 2 Timothy 4:7 he reports: "I have fought the good fight, I have finished the race, I have kept the faith."

Witnesses—rope-holders—give us encouragement and help us finish well, if we will let them.

2. We Must Face Our Impediments

In Hebrews 12 we are told to throw off everything that hinders us. Everything. For the paralytic, that meant doing whatever it took to get off his mat. If you were the paralytic, what would you have been thinking? Maybe: *These guys are going to drop me. I'll add a concussion to my obvious problems.* Or perhaps: *I am so embarrassed. Surely the owner of this home is going to throw us out.* Or possibly: *My friends really love me. I am grateful for their compassion.*

Whatever our thoughts, it is imperative that we face whatever gets in the way of running well. Consider the following list of impediments that might be keeping you from running ahead into more intimacy with God. Check the ones that apply to you.

___ Bitterness	___ Busyness	___ Comparisons
___ Competitiveness	___ Complaining	___ Control
___ Critical spirit	___ Deception	___ Depression
___ Discouragement	___ Disobedience	___ Distractions
___ Doubt	___ Embarrassment	___ Expectations
___ Fear	___ Hurt	___ Indifference
___ Lack of Focus	___ Laziness	___ Pride
___ Procrastination	___ Unbelief	___ Unforgiveness
___ Sin	___ "Religious," self-righteous spirit	
___ Unwillingness	___ Other _____	

Sometimes the things that keep us on our mats are not heart attitudes but people. Paul's question in Galatians 5:7 is crucial: "You were running a good race. Who cut in on you and kept you from obeying the truth?" The paralytic's friends could not take him to Jesus through the front door "because of the crowd." Who was in the crowd? A lot of Pharisees and teachers of the law. They had come from every village of Galilee, so the place was teeming with them (see Luke 5:17–19). They were a religious lot. I bet when tile chips and clay bits started falling and sunlight peeked through the roof, they would have been the first ones to shout about disrespect. They probably demanded that somebody fix the roof. Now.

John Fischer makes this observation in *12 Steps for the Recovering Pharisee* (Bethany House, 2000):

Let's face it, it's a heavy burden being a Pharisee: managing truth, defending God, stalking heresy, enforcing the rules, and keeping those out of the kingdom who do not belong there. Long faces, long robes, long ledgers, long lists.

3. We Have One Predominant Snare

If you are like me, you probably checked several items on the list. But there is usually one that ensnares more easily than all the others combined. Have you spotted yours? If not, ask God to show you what it is. For me it is bitterness. I recognize this as a generational sin but one I need to be responsible to hand over to the Lord. Allow me to explain.

I had been out for a delightful dinner with one of my rope-holders—an accountability partner. We spent the evening enjoying fine food for our stomachs and our souls. Then on the way to the parking lot she said, "I'm reluctant to mention this, Marilyn, because I don't want to be harsh. But, I think you have some bitterness in your heart."

I was shocked. First of all, I looked—to my shame—for bitterness in her. Second, I did not ask for her counsel, at least not that night. Third, the evening had gone so well. *How could she wreck everything?* It did not take long, however, to turn my irritation into an honest question for God: "Is she right? Show me if there is any bitterness in me."

Be careful what you ask God, because He will answer. For two weeks I heard nothing. I thought I was off the hook. But then it happened. I was at a cabin by myself finishing a writing deadline. I had worked hard all day, so I turned the computer off and turned the television on. That night I listened to a message given by Adrian Rogers on a Christian television program. He said, "Tonight, we will talk about"—you guessed it—"bitterness." From that point on it was as if we were having a dialogue. Dr. Rogers was inside the tube and I was outside, but he consistently answered all the questions my heart raised.

He talked of Hebrews 12:15: "See to it that no one misses the grace of God and that no bitter root grows up to cause trouble and defile many." Dr. Rogers said that seeds and soil are needed for any root to grow. Usually a root of bitterness is from a seed of hurt. And the hurt most often comes from someone close to you. If it is not a close relationship, the hurt is not as intense. The soil harbors the hurt and the root grows.

I was still in a state of denial. "I just don't see that I am bitter, Lord. Help me to understand."

It was then that Adrian Rogers said, "Let me help you understand if you are harboring a hurt in the soil of your heart. Have there been any negative thoughts about any person or situation for several days in the last two weeks?" I was nailed. I could easily identify the person and what she had said. She was a close friend and a follower of Jesus. I rehearsed how it had hurt me. I was bitter and the root was growing; little tentacles of defilement were digging deeper into the soil of my heart.

My next question was audible. "What do I do about this?"

Dr. Rogers did not disappoint me. Again the answer came. It was as if God was speaking directly through his lips. He outlined three points: (1) Let God reveal it; (2) Let grace remove it; and (3) Let good replace it.

God had already revealed it. My accountability partner had voiced it, and now the Lord Himself was pointing it out gently, but firmly.

The speaker explained that we run into difficulty with this problem because we try to handle it on our own. I could identify with that, too. I had done all the "right" things. I had tried to serve her, deciding that I would be the "more mature" of us both. But I was doing it all in my flesh. The truth is, Dr. Rogers explained, only grace can remove it. I realized then that my part of the equation was to admit that I was helpless to get rid of the bitterness. I simply needed to surrender to Jesus' touch.

My next question became obvious. "What does the good look like that can replace this ugly thing?"

God continued to answer through Dr. Rogers' teaching. First, He instructed me to pray for the one who had hurt me, and He was not interested in prayers intended to fix her. He wanted some honest, caring intercession on her behalf. Do you know how hard it is to stay angry with someone you are earnestly praying for?

Second, God invited me to ask Him how I had done the very things I was upset with her about. I allowed Him to examine my heart. He showed me my unsavory places and it gave me compassion—not anger—for her. I was guilty of the same things.

Third, God told me that this was not a cause for woe. This very problem was one of the things He designed to get me to focus on Him, to seek Him with intimacy. It was a cause for praise. My heart began to sing, and by doing these three things every time the nasty thoughts came, the bitterness soon began to wither and fade away.

As God cemented these truths into my heart, I pondered the precedent of others in Scripture who had been disappointed with God's people. Moses was not pleased on hearing the revelry of the calf worshipers as he came down the mountain. Job was disturbed about the uncaring platitudes of his windbag friends. And Jesus had to be disappointed that His three closest disciples could not stay awake for even a short time as He agonized in the garden. The exciting thing, though, was that the disappointment motivated Moses, Job and Jesus to seek the face of the Father with more intensity than before. And the same thing was happening with me.

Just to be sure I got it, God offered another caveat. I was listening to a tape by Francis Frangipane. He was telling of the time his daughter asked him and his wife to care for a rare pet bird while she was away. They agreed. On the first night, Francis put his hand in the cage to feed the bird. The unexpected occurred. The feathered Gestapo flew down and pecked at his hand so ferociously that it bled. Francis tried again. And even a third time. No luck. The bird remained too frightened to behave decently.

Francis gave up, but his wife did not. Faithfully, she fed the bird, washing and bandaging her new wounds that the bird's sharp beak inflicted. Finally, after a few weeks, the bird started eating out of her hand. Frangipane then said words that brought an audible gasp from the depths of my heart. He said, "So by my wife's wounds, that bird was healed."

I am not sure that the lesson I learned was the one intended by the speaker, but God used his words to address my need. I asked God aloud, "Does that mean that by my wounds, someone else could be healed—if I asked You?" There was a resounding yes.

Now, whenever a sharp new wound is inflicted on my heart or an old wound festers—by a report that shades the truth or a continuing jab at my feelings or an unwelcome lecture in the obvious—I use it as a call to prayer. "Lord

God, I feel wounded again. Please use my hurt to heal the other person and me."

Would you dare ask God to do the same thing for you? Ask Him to turn your wounds into healing. Ask Him to reveal what is keeping you on your mat. Admit that you are helpless before whatever it is. Beg Him for His grace to remove it. And let Him replace your lurking entanglements with good of His design.

4. The Race Is Marked Out

Lots of folks train at gyms or spas. Fewer people have personal trainers, but those who do could testify to the value of such a focused approach to meeting their personal fitness needs. Some people need work on their abs. Some on their hips. Some need help to overcome an injury or illness. Personal trainers avoid anything that would bring harm to their clients while helping them achieve their goals.

God is your personal trainer. The race He marks out for you is unique to you. Whatever has come into your path is His complete and perfect design for you. His plan offers much. "'For I know the plans I have for you,' declares the Lord, 'plans to prosper you and not to harm you, plans to give you hope and a future'" (Jeremiah 29:11).

There are no formulas for intimacy. There are no prescribed rules for dealing with things that try to trip us in the race. What worked for me was His design for me. Perhaps He will use some of my journey to help guide yours, but He will most assuredly do it in a different way. In *My Utmost for His Highest*, Oswald Chambers warns: "Never make a principle out of your experience; let God be as original with other people as He is with you."

5. The Goal Must Be Clear

First Corinthians 9:24–26 poses a viable question:

Do you not know that in a race all the runners run, but only one gets the prize? Run in such a way as to get the prize. Everyone who competes in the games goes into strict training. They do it to get a crown that will not last; but we do it to get a crown that will last forever. Therefore I do not run like a man running aimlessly.

Make no mistake. The direction is heavenward and the prize is God the Father, the Son and the Holy Spirit. My friend Cheryl Stephens succumbed to ovarian cancer at 47. She understood that Jesus was the goal. Consider her words:

Remember me not for who I was
But for who Jesus was in me.
Remember me not for the things I've done
But for the things Jesus did through me.
Remember me not as one who loved
Without remembering that "He first loved me."
Remember me not as one who gave
But one to whom much was given.
Remember me not as one who spoke of God
But as one who knew God through His Son, Jesus.
Remember me not as one who prayed
But remember the One to whom I prayed.
Remember me not as one who was strong
But as one who cried out to God to be my strength.
Remember me not as one who died
But as one who lives forever because I have believed.
Remember not my life and death
For they will profit you nothing.

But please . . . please remember the life and death of
   Jesus.
For He gave His life that we might live.
He died that we might never have to and He rose again
That we might have eternal life.
Remember not me, but do remember Jesus.

In the account of the paralytic, Jesus was center stage. He
was the goal. And I believe He was jumping up and down
and clapping because somebody got it. Somebody wanted
His touch and the transformation that brings. Only He
can direct us in the race and cause us to see His face in the
process. Only He can heal our attitudes and forgive our sins.
There is only one goal. It is Jesus.

Paul knew it well. He said:

> I consider everything a loss compared to the surpassing
> greatness of knowing Christ Jesus my Lord, for whose sake
> I have lost all things. I consider them rubbish, that I may
> gain Christ. . . . Forgetting what is behind and straining
> toward what is ahead, I press on toward the goal to win
> the prize for which God has called me heavenward in
> Christ Jesus.
>
> Philippians 3:8, 13–14

Forget what is behind. Strain toward what is ahead.
Press on. The prize is near. Once you are freed from your
entanglements, you can be freed for intimacy with God.
Freed from to be freed for. You will be amazed. You will
praise Him. You will be in awe. You will run the race well.
And you will echo the sentiment of those watching the
paralytic, "[I] have seen remarkable things today" (Luke
5:26).

Searching for More

1. Where are you?

　　　　 _____ On your mat
　　　　 _____ Being carried by your friends
　　　　 _____ Right in front of Jesus
　　　　 _____ Standing up
　　　　 _____ Picking up what you have been lying on
　　　　 _____ Praising God
　　　　 _____ Holding the ropes for someone else

2. Who have been the rope-holders in your life? How will you thank them?
3. Whom are you a rope-holder for, placing him or her right in front of Jesus?
4. What is your greatest snare? What keeps you from letting God reveal it, allowing grace to remove it and seeing what good could replace it? Are you ready to surrender it?

5

Throwing Off Hindrances

*S*et my spirit free!"

That was my heart cry for three and a half years. Realizing there were things wrong in my life, I begged God for help. Key relationships seemed to be crumbling. Anger erupted out of nowhere, spewing hateful ashes and bitter resentment. I felt used and abused, as though I was walking on hot sand with no shoes. I was miserable.

Admittedly I was more concerned about how to get relief from my problems than I was about the growing chasm between the Lord and me. All the while, God was still using me in a speaking and writing ministry and I met my days with reasonable energy. But I knew something was not right, so I continued my heart roar. "Set my spirit free!" I demanded. It was more persistent now, often accompanied with a pounding fist and a stomping foot.

Expecting a great, galloping, noisy sin to make itself known, I waited and watched. But only the daily variety of skirmishes with darkness seemed to beg confession. All the while my marriage was growing stale and I seethed over my perceptions of others' attitudes toward me. I struggled with jealousy. I also had a problem putting boundaries around my life. "No" was what I longed to say when I did not want to do whatever was asked, but "Yes" was what I heard coming from my lips.

About that time my husband and I invited a young woman to come live with us. Cindy had finished training in counseling with Larry Crabb at Colorado Christian University and desired to set up a practice within our church fellowship. Our part of the Body of Christ was two thousand miles away from her current location in Colorado, so we offered free room and board to help her get launched into ministry. Just about the time I was priding myself on the good deed we were doing for her, a stark realization came: God had provided a personal, live-in counselor for me!

And, frankly, that did not help my attitude.

This realization came after a phone call—a long-distance call I had placed to my mom. The conversation, difficult as always, had dragged on with her usual put-downs and guilt manipulators. I had heard the all-too-familiar litany of all the ways I had not met whatever was her latest expectation of me. I hung up the phone and screeched disapproval.

"That woman is going to drive me nuts." I had had it, and I voiced my displeasure with pathos, a combination of sorrow and pity.

Our new houseguest was quiet for a time and then spoke carefully chosen words. "I've overheard some of the conversations with your mother," Cindy said kindly.

I looked at her with a less-than-pleased expression.

She continued: "I think you're looking for something from your mother that she might never be able to give you.

And, if you could figure out what that is—and I don't know what it is—I think God will set your spirit free."

Quite possibly, that may have been the only time in my life when I looked like a raging bull. You know. Eyes wide. Nostrils flaring. Smoke spewing from my ears. I was mad. You might think I would be grateful for Cindy's concern, but, no, I was definitely mad.

How dare she? I thought. My emotions were churning. *I dealt with "the mother issue" long ago, thank you. Besides, "advice not asked for is criticism," and I certainly did not ask.*

But Cindy's words had hit a target. She could not have known that the prayer I had been echoing for more than three years contained the very words she chose to say at that moment, *Set my spirit free.* So after a week of fussing, I decided that praying might be a better move. The words did not come easily.

"Lord, if my relationship with my mother is why my spirit is in chains, show me what I'm looking for from her that she can't give me." Then came the hardest part. Waiting and listening.

Keeping an ear out for God to speak became more difficult than I could have imagined. Days turned into weeks. Weeks lagged and became months. But still I listened, confident God would speak the truth to me.

His voice came one evening while I was listening to a speaker at a weekend retreat. She was sharing her story of how God had helped her forgive her father after years of dysfunctional relating.

As I listened to her words, it was almost like hearing my own story. Painful childhood details, memories of offenses—destructive words, deep hurts, unfulfilled expectations—were still close to the surface. The speaker continued her story, explaining how she had finally dealt with her bitterness and how that action had pushed her to yield to God. It was surrender, she said, that gave her freedom.

In my mind I reviewed my own struggle with bitterness and my decision to forgive. I did not feel the need to retrace steps that were washed with my own tears of surrender. *I've been there,* I thought, *and done that. And I don't need to go there again.*

But in spite of myself, my eye was drawn to one page of my notes and a big set of parentheses that seemed to appear there independently of my own design. That is to say, my hand moved the pen but God seemed to create the words. In the parentheses waiting there on the page, I wrote: *Could it just be that the thing you're looking for from your mother is one unselfish moment, when she could put you above her own interests?*

The question stung. Could it be?

I pondered it for a moment and then transported myself back to the seminar. In ping-pong fashion I bounced back and forth between the speaker's voice, then further questions from the Lord, then back to the speaker, and then back to more personal issues.

Could it be that the reason you get angry quickly is because you perceive—real or imagined—that peoples' words and actions toward you are selfish—just like your mom's?

And, further, could it be that sometimes—not always, but sometimes—you serve people with your hands but not your heart because you think it would be selfish of you not to?

These were perplexing challenges, but, since the weekend was packed with activities, this was not the time to analyze what they meant. In short, I could not spend much time thinking about these questions until returning home Sunday evening. After my husband greeted me, he sat down and patted the place beside him as an invitation to come and share the events of the weekend with him. I began telling him the contents of the big parentheses when I burst into tears.

The crying took me by surprise and, when I could catch my breath, I asked John the million-dollar question. "Do you think wanting one unselfish moment from Mother, where she would put me above herself, is what I'm looking for?"

John was quiet for several uncomfortable minutes. When I finally looked up, his eyes were wet, too.

"I know that's what it is," he said gently.

"How can you be so sure?"

With tears spilling on his cheeks, he said, "Because your spirit toward me is different."

That was the most intimate moment of our marriage. We cried together and hugged for a long time. Then the conversation turned to lighter things.

"What are your marching orders, Mal?" John knew that whether I went on a retreat as a participant or the leader, I always asked God to clear a new path, to show me how He wanted me to proceed on the basis of what I had heard from Him.

"Fasting is the direction God wants me to take," I told John confidently. "I think God wants me to pray and fast about this whole 'mother thing.' So I'm going to start tomorrow morning." And with a dramatic flourish I added, "I'll fast until I get an answer." Mercifully, God gave me a response by lunchtime.

Monday mornings are usually tough enough without having to deal with a heavy topic. But the dawn of this Monday was different. I could hardly wait to hear what God would say to my heart.

So armed with my Bible, my easy chair and a cup of tea, I began the dialogue with God that changed my life. It was as if God smiled broadly at the first glimpse of me, and He invited me to sit in His lap immediately. He was about to free me from this difficulty in order to free me for intimacy with Him.

As usual, I spoke first. "Where should we begin, Lord?"

Not knowing the direction to take, I began by reading the portion of God's Word that defines His chosen fast. Isaiah 58 proved to be just the place to start. Snuggling in the Father's embrace, I watched as He underlined verses six and nine with His finger. Just for me.

> "Is not this the kind of fasting I have chosen: to loose the chains of injustice and untie the cords of the yoke, to set the oppressed free and break every yoke? . . . Then you will call, and the LORD will answer; you will cry for help, and he will say: Here am I. If you do away with the yoke of oppression, with the pointing finger and malicious talk."

I did not know much about yokes. I just knew my spirit was not free and it felt as though something heavy was on my shoulders, pushing my head low. And it had been there for a very long time.

"What does all this mean?" I begged.

My answers came, in part, from a commentary where I learned some things about yokes. A yoke is a wooden frame that holds a pair of draft animals, like oxen, together for service to their master. The frame, which fits over the necks of the beasts, is shaped like a capital *B* on its side, with a bar positioned through the top to hold it secure. Then cords are tied around the animals' necks to hold the yoke in place.

It made sense that if a yoke were to be removed, the opposite procedure would be employed. In reversing the order, the cords would be untied first, then the rod removed and then the wooden yoke lifted off.

Looking at the Isaiah 58 verses again, I was astonished to note that "loosening chains" was God's intent. Convinced that I was on the right track, I again reviewed verse nine. Certainly the cries to set my spirit free qualified as a call to God. And, oh, how welcome the promises were! He will answer. He will say: "Here am I."

I wanted desperately to fling off the yoke of oppression, but I was timid to ask the Lord about my "pointing finger and malicious talk." He gently but firmly reminded me of the many times I had harbored resentful thoughts and exhibited rude actions. They all added up to a lot of unforgiveness and bitterness on my part. But I was being summoned to a loving Father who wanted to touch and heal me, not reporting to the always disappointed earthly parent who would most assuredly scold and punish.

As I took steps closer, the light dawned brighter and I noted a comforting sense of warmth. I asked Him what this all meant. "How could yokes have anything to do with my heart cry?" It was then the deliverance took place, much like a bird being released from a cage or an animal from a net.

God began, *When Cindy shared that you might be looking for something your mom couldn't do for you, that was Me . . . untying the cords of your yoke. I do want to set your spirit free.*

When you filled the big parentheses with words at the retreat, that was Me . . . breaking the rod of the yoke over My knee.

And when you and John wept together, that was Me . . . removing the yoke!

Oh, how I cried! Sweet tears. Tears of release. Refreshing tears. Tears of restoration. Happy tears. Free tears. Really . . . free tears.

But the unchained tears turned swiftly to terrified ones.

"I don't know how to live without the yoke that has kept my spirit overwhelmed, my shoulders sagging and my head low. This is uncharted territory, Lord. Help me. Please."

Struggling to understand it all, I asked question after question and God answered. As He touched the place of intense hurt, I began to see my mother with new eyes. I began to understand that she had done the best she knew to do. She was a wild child with a prodigal's heart. It occurred to me that she never allowed anyone to touch her own wounded places, especially not Jesus. So all she could do was pass hurts on.

I have discovered that people who have never really been heard, cannot easily hear others. I wondered how hurtful it must have been for my mother rarely to have had a listening ear tune into her deepest concerns. That insight alone gave me more compassion than anger for her. God spoke authority and comfort into my heart.

I can honestly say that this deliverance—this yoke removal—not only set me free but also released my mother. Without words from me, Mom changed before her death. She became more able than ever before to show a caring attitude about the heart concerns, the time commitments and the general well-being of others. The Holy Spirit had touched her, too. I will say a little more about that in the next chapter, but it is indeed true that when you forgive another person, you set two prisoners free: the one forgiven and yourself.

How is it that I could learn life lessons on deliverance and pass the test of "Yoke Removal 101" with excellence? It is only because Jesus did the course work and He took the final. All I did was surrender to His tutelage. God saw my misery. He heard me crying out for help and He came down to rescue me from an oppressive hand. Then He brought me up out of that place into a good and spacious place, full of freedom.

Do I pass the test every day, living with the light, easy yoke? No, certainly not.

But I had learned from the Bible commentary that carpenters in Bible times used their wood most often to construct plows and yokes. And when I remembered that Jesus was a carpenter, it was as though God settled my soul into a warm bubble bath. I breathed a deep, relaxing breath as I realized that for 53 years Jesus had been fashioning a light yoke just for me. Matthew 11:28–30 took on special meaning:

> "Come to me, all you who are weary and burdened, and I will give you rest. Take my yoke upon you and learn from me, for I am gentle and humble in heart, and you will find rest for your souls. For my yoke is easy and my burden is light."

God was indeed—at long last—"[bestowing] glory on me and [lifting] up my head" (Psalm 3:3). No longer did I have to live in resignation to the bondage that hindered my race; now I could live delivered. In resignation the door had been open but I did not know I could fly out of the trap. In deliverance I was invited, shown how and prodded to put my hand in His faithful grip. He made me aware that the gate was open, and I could fly away and be at rest.

The strain now is learning to live with the replaced light yoke—serving with both my hands and heart and refusing to rewind negative thought tapes. I need to press on, knowing that God has indeed released my spirit from the bondage that had hindered me and left me captured, suffocating and paralyzed all these decades.

I know that I need not respond to the negative patterns others choose to follow. They no longer have to affect me adversely. And, now that selfishness is defined in a healthy way, I no longer need to march to someone else's cadence. I still appreciate the approval of others, but now I do not need it to move ahead. I need only the Father's approval. Further, even though I was not nurtured as a child I am able to nurture freely. How? Christ is an apt tutor.

So now what? How are things today? Are the injured relationships healed? It has been said that godliness is not an event, but a process. It takes time. I have not been set free so much as I am being set free.

Now much less time elapses between living the old way and allowing God to replace the heavy with the light; the bitter with the sweet. I get a chance more often now to lift my head and smile, to "soar on wings like eagles" (Isaiah 40:31). I have been freed from the old so that I can be freed for God to dream through the new me.

And so can you. The hindrance that you need to throw off may not be a family issue. Perhaps it is something from your past or a bad habit that begs transformation. Maybe it is an abuse issue or a problem with one of your children. Perhaps yours is a health difficulty or the attitudes of others that you have no control over. Maybe you are in financial bondage. Maybe you do not know what it is, but you sense that there is something holding you back from the intimacy you desire with God.

Whatever it is, known or unknown at this point, God offers freedom. He knows what it is and He wants you to be able to run the race with ease. The spiritual reality for me was that I needed to surrender my expectations of my mother to God. That dysfunctional lifestyle demanded yielding before the marathon toward intimacy with God would move forward.

Surrender is nothing more than taking our white-knuckled grip off of our lives and opening our hands to God. Allow me to explain in the next chapter.

Searching for More

1. Is there evidence that something is not right in your life? Staleness? Jealousy? Paranoia? Excessive busyness?
2. Whom has God sent your way to get you out of the muck and mire?
3. Share about a time when forgiveness set you and another person free.
4. Where is "the pointing finger and malicious talk" evident in your life?
5. Share a time when God was "the glory and the lifter of your head."

6

The Sin That Entangles

When our son Mark was a toddler he loved to sit on the stool at the breakfast bar between the kitchen and the dining room. He would wobble over, grasp the spindles and flail himself against the stool, trying to get his chubby, little legs on the seat. Of course, he could not do it. Not without help. I tried many times to get him to let go his grip on the stool so I could lift him up, but to Mark that meant certain death of the dream. His determined expression said it all: "Let go? Are you crazy?" When he finally did release his grip, I could lift him up. Then he found himself where he wanted to be all along.

Do you do the same thing with your life situations? Holding on white-knuckled, sure that if you open your hand you will never attain your goal? I do. I forget that surrender to God is an open hand. It is a quiet "Yes, Lord."

Through the many lessons God taught me in my relationship with my mother, I began to understand why we find it hard to surrender. It is because we are holding on to expectations and we dare not let go. Perhaps you have never considered how dangerous expectations can be. And what do expectations have to do with sin?

Simply this: Expectations turn our steps away from the race God has called us to run and put us straight on the path to pride. It is a subtle deception, this bending toward sin, because our expectations seem so natural. But it is a stronghold, and we need to be set free. Otherwise when we focus on our expectations, when we hold on to our own determination, and our own agenda, we miss God. It has been said that expectations are premeditated resentments. Resentments fueled by pride. Certainly that happened to the Pharisees. They rejected Jesus because He did not look like what they expected and He exposed their prideful ways.

Expectations have a "me" focus. They pop up when we think we are owed something. "I deserve more" is the accompanying heart cry. (Sometimes folks with the biggest entourage and the most possessions have the biggest expectations.) Usually our expectations are too high for ourselves and others and too low for God. Then when difficult situations come, we say, "I can't wait for God. I must move ahead without Him." That is not our intention, but, nonetheless, that is what we sometimes do.

A sure way to know if you are grasping an inappropriate expectation is to observe your reaction when the expectation is not met. When false expectations are not met, we usually become angry. The problem is that "man's anger does not bring about the righteous life that God desires" (James 1:20). If we were exhibiting righteous anger, that would mean one of God's goals was being blocked, not ours.

In his introduction to the book of Joel in *The Message*, Eugene Peterson explains:

There is a sense in which catastrophe doesn't introduce anything new into our lives. It simply exposes the moral or spiritual reality that already exists but was hidden beneath an overlay of routine, self-preoccupation, and business as usual. Then suddenly, there it is before us: a moral universe in which our accumulated decisions—on what we say and do, on how we treat others, on whether or not we will obey God's commands—are set in the stark light of God's judgment.

There is an account in the Bible that makes this image visible. It shows the entanglement of pride and the value of surrendered expectations in a man facing a catastrophe. It is found in 2 Kings 5:1–15 and it is about Naaman.

The Cast of Characters

This is a story of one man's learning to lay aside the sin that so easily entangles. Naaman's story is told through the appearance of an unusual cast of characters. Let's begin with Naaman, himself.

1. Naaman

Naaman was an army commander, and a valiant one at that. He had power over many others and he himself was under the authority of the king of Aram. His king held him in high regard because Naaman had won countless victories for the pagan nation. Naaman had lots of things going for him. He was wealthy and he was loyal. He seemed able to listen to others, even those beneath him, but he had one overriding problem: He was a leper. And his pride prodded him to set up personal expectations, as we will see.

2. Naaman's Wife

The woman in the account is unnamed but important. She had servants and she was a good listener. An Israelite girl had just been captured by bands from Aram and placed in her charge. The girl voiced a worthy plea: "If only my master would see the prophet who is in Samaria! He would cure him of his leprosy" (2 Kings 5:3).

This woman obviously wanted what was good for her husband and she communicated well with him. She told him what the girl had said and Naaman checked it out with his own master, the king of Aram.

3. The Servant Girl

This youngster is also unnamed. I find her extraordinary. Think of it. She had just been taken from her people and her homeland and placed in service in a pagan land. She had many reasons to be bitter and angry, and yet she was considering the well-being of her new master. What a godly Hebrew girl! No resentment, just compassion.

Her first line of hope was spiritual. Her method of operation was this: If you have a problem, you go to a man of God for help. And she knew where to find such a man. She looked past the appearance of her new master and the fact that he had taken her away from her own family, and she saw his need. What is more, she had a desire to do something about it.

4. The King of Aram

Here was a man in charge, a can-do kind of fellow. I am sure he had a swagger, but it seemed coupled with a compassionate and caring side. When Naaman told him what the girl from Israel had said, the king immediately told him to go on the journey and he sent a letter along to the king of Israel on Naaman's behalf. His first line of hope was political and military.

Second Kings 5:18 tells us that he worshiped the pagan god Rimmon. This was the god of the thunder and the storm, perfect for a warrior desiring lightning speed and thunderous results in his conquests. It appears that his name may have been Ben-hadad, fashioned after his god.

5. The King of Israel

Talk about a man with paranoia. When he read the letter that the king of Aram had sent to him, "he tore his robes and said, 'Am I God? Can I kill and bring back to life? Why does this fellow send someone to me to be cured of his leprosy? See how he is trying to pick a quarrel with me!'" (2 Kings 5:7).

This was a demonstrative king. He tore his robes as a sign of despair and grief on a regular basis. And he had quite a history of not wanting to get involved in helping others (see 2 Kings 6:26–33).

It appears that this king may have been Joram, the son of King Ahab and Queen Jezebel, which would explain quite a lot. He reigned for twelve years and during the first five years of Judah's King Jehoshaphat. The Scriptures are clear about him: "He did evil in the eyes of the LORD" (2 Kings 3:2).

6. Elisha

Elisha was a prophet in Israel, the one mentored by Elijah himself. He lived in Samaria and had servants and messengers in his employ. He knew how to give directions.

But there is something important he did not pick up from his mentor. In 2 Kings 5:8 we read that he heard about the Israelite king's reaction to the situation and sent him this message: "Have the man [Naaman] come to me and he will know that there is a prophet in Israel." Elisha's focus was on himself as God's agent.

Look at the difference in the words his tutor, Elijah, prayed during his contest with the prophets of Baal:

"O LORD, God of Abraham, Isaac and Israel, let it be known today that you are God in Israel and that I am your servant and have done all these things at your command. Answer me, O LORD, answer me, so these people will know that you, O LORD, are God, and that you are turning their hearts back again."

1 Kings 18:36–37

Elijah's focus was on the God of Israel. That is very different from a gaze directed at a prophet.

Naaman got the message and with his full entourage arrived at Elisha's door. Elisha did not come out to greet him, however, but sent a messenger to tell the great warrior to go wash in the Jordan seven times and he would be healed.

Here is where we see Naaman's expectations in full light. Naaman was angry at this message and possibly felt snubbed. In 2 Kings 5:11, Naaman said: "I thought that he would surely" do such and such. Then he "went off in a rage" (verse 12).

Be honest. Have you ever caught yourself saying, "Well, I thought that she would surely . . ."? That line reveals unmet expectations.

7. Naaman's Servants

Last but not least are the attendants Naaman brought along with him. They approached Naaman in his anger. These men risked rejection and possibly their lives by speaking the truth in love. The way they addressed their master, though, leads me to believe they had a good relationship with him. "My father," they said, "if the prophet had told you to do some great thing, would you not have done it? How much more, then, when he tells you, 'Wash and be cleansed'!" (2 Kings 5:13).

Naaman listened. And he surrendered his pride. He "went down and dipped himself in the Jordan" (2 Kings 5:14) as he had been told and he was cleansed.

Naaman's Expectations

In this story there are at least six unmet expectations that fueled Naaman's ire.

1. The Time Expectation

In 2 Kings 5:5 we are told that on his journey to Samaria, Naaman took with him silver and gold and "ten sets of clothing." Perhaps he had in mind that the excursion would take about ten days to get the job of healing done.

Do you have time expectations? Are you perhaps angry because something either happened too soon or not soon enough? The author of all time would be pleased for you to open your hand and surrender your time issue to Him.

2. The Position Expectation

Have you ever been in a place where you thought that surely the people in charge would be more honoring of your title or your standing in the community or church? Do you require recognition of your role of authority in any setting? If you do, then perhaps you would have been like Naaman.

Elisha sent a messenger out to this VIP and Naaman was enraged. "I thought that he would surely come out to me" (2 Kings 5:11). Naaman's position, in his eyes, demanded that the head honcho do the work, not some no-account underling.

3. The Personality Expectation

The text continues in 2 Kings 5:11 to say: "I thought that he would surely come out to me and stand. . . ." The original Hebrew word for *stand* has the tone of confidence and self-assurance. It signifies a stance of authority.

Do you think that only the in-charge kinds of people can accomplish God's bidding in your life? Do you wait for the can-do models that shine with certainty? Or might the ordinary ones sent with the power of our extraordinary God sometimes do the job best?

4. The Procedural Expectation

In that same verse, 2 Kings 5:11, Naaman continued his complaint: "I thought that he would surely come out to me and stand and call on the name of the LORD his God, wave his hand over the spot and cure me of my leprosy."

Not only did Naaman want to be healed, he wanted the man of God to do it his way. Apparently, the warrior had a procedure all mapped out in his head and when it did not happen that way, there was trouble to be had.

This is something like wanting your child to do the chores assigned to him, but you want him to do the work your way. Sometimes his way works better. But, no, it must be done your way.

This is a matter of control. Might this be something you need to surrender?

God has His own idea of procedure, and sometimes it conflicts with our method of operation. For an example of such a problem see 2 Samuel 6 and 1 Chronicles 13 and 15.

5. The Complexity Expectation

Naaman had a complex problem. Leprosy is a debilitating disease that carries with it a social and emotional stigma, much like AIDS. Because it was such a difficult situation, Naaman assumed that the solution to his problem had to be complex, too. So when the answer suggested by the man of God seemed so simple, it threw him into a maelstrom.

The instructions were to "go, wash yourself seven times in the Jordan" (2 Kings 5:10).

"What? Surely, you're kidding."

Perhaps you, too, consistently make things more difficult than they need to be. Your God is bigger than any situation you may find yourself in at the moment and He can sort it all out. Do not allow this to get in the way of growing in intimacy with Him.

6. The "Familiar Formula" Expectation

Once again, Naaman wanted things his own way. He expected that what was familiar and had always worked before would be the formula for now as well. He had relied on his wealth, his position, his strength, his entourage and his connections. It had always worked before, why should this time be different? He could not understand why the resources of his own land were not good enough. "'Are not Abana and Pharpar, the rivers of Damascus, better than any of the waters of Israel? Couldn't I wash in them and be cleansed?' So he turned and went off in a rage" (2 Kings 5:12).

Do you expect that the same programs done in the same way will pull you out of whatever situation you are in at the moment? Is your first line of hope spiritual? Or is it really political, relational or judicial? After all, in our society it is the norm to sue anytime something does not go our way. We are a litigious lot.

God rarely does the same thing exactly the same way in two separate lives or in two differing circumstances. You are so unique and treasured by Him that He will touch your life in new and exciting ways. You do not need the pressure of expected formulas. You should not hide behind the familiar. There are rarely ten steps to success in any endeavor. Allow God to do a new thing. The prophet Isaiah underscores God's intent: "Forget the former things; do not dwell on the past. See, I am doing a new thing! Now it springs up; do you not perceive it? I am making a way in the desert and streams in the wasteland" (Isaiah 43:18–19).

God showed Himself strong in Naaman's story. He revealed Himself to the warrior as the stream of cleansing in his leprous wasteland—the living water. Elisha was going to show him that there was a prophet in Israel, but Naaman's pronouncement at the end indicates that God's name and renown won the day: "He [Naaman] stood before him and said, 'Now I know that there is no God in all the world except in Israel'" (2 Kings 5:15). Naaman's eyes had seen the true God and this God did indeed restore his flesh. But He did even more. When Naaman let go of the sin that had entangled his life, God cleansed his soul, too.

Naaman learned that God expected obedience from him. God longs for obedience from you, too. Why? Because He wants to bless you and He knows that blessing comes through

97

obedience. So consider: Will you obey His call to surrender? Romans 12:1–2 in *The Message* says it well:

> God helping you: Take your everyday, ordinary life—your sleeping, eating, going-to-work, and walking-around life— and place it before God as an offering. Embracing what God does for you is the best thing you can do for him. Don't become so well-adjusted to your culture that you fit into it without even thinking. Instead, fix your attention on God. You'll be changed from the inside out.

Closure At Last

In regard to my mother, I fell for every one of the expectations Naaman exhibited. I was impatient for a solution. I assigned positions: Mom—unredeemed; me—saved and on higher ground. I fussed about our personality differences and made things more complex than they often were. I wanted things done my way, mostly with words and familiar patterns. But God worked without words in His timing and did a work of wonder.

Because of the change God worked in my own heart, I found myself grateful for the opportunity to be with my mother the last month of her life. We knew the end was near. It was not an easy time because death is ugly. This woman whose whole life was centered on appearance became unsightly as her time to leave this earth drew near. She had always been stunningly beautiful. Five feet ten inches tall. One hundred and twenty-eight pounds. Blonde. Lithe. Fun-spirited.

What I noticed, however, was that as her body withered, her spirit flourished. Her appearance was anything but attractive, but her spirit was sweet. For the first time in my life she said the two things I had forever longed to hear: "God bless you" and "You are beautiful to me." I had never voiced that longing, but with my surrender of expectations—my open hand—God touched the desires of my heart and hers.

On the last day of Mom's life, she could not speak. Her eyes followed me everywhere I went in the room. Just the night before, I had been reading about the reconciliation of Jacob and Esau and marveling over the words in Genesis 33:10: "To see your face is like seeing the face of God." As my mother's gaze intensified on me, I prayed that as she saw my face it would be like seeing the face of God and that forgiveness would be written all over it.

She cried out to God in her last year and I believe that this one who loved to dance wildly is twirling with Him right now. Forgiven. Whole. Loved. Understood. Heard. Free. And me? I am getting rid of hindrances and learning to have fewer expectations of myself and others and more of our powerful God. God has set my spirit free to run, day after day, deeper into this dimension of His love. He wants to set your spirit free, too.

Will you open your hands to Him?

Searching for More

1. When have you ever said: "I thought that he/she would surely have . . . "? What is your perspective on that situation now?
2. When you have a need, what is your first line of hope most often?

___ Military   ___ Political   ___ Judicial
___ Familial   ___ Spiritual   ___ Relational

3. Which of the cast of characters do you most identify with and why?

_____ Naaman
_____ Naaman's wife
_____ The servant girl
_____ The king of Aram
_____ The king of Israel
_____ Elisha
_____ Naaman's servants

4. What kinds of expectations do you most easily fall prey to?

_____ Time
_____ Position
_____ Personality
_____ Complexity
_____ Procedure
_____ Familiar formula
_____ Other

5. What do you think God wants you to release from your white-knuckled grip? How will you offer Him your open hand?

PART 3

higher

The Mountain of God

The Lord descended to the top of Mount Sinai and called Moses to the top of the mountain. So Moses went up.

Exodus 19:20

7

Nobody Descends to the Top

Four days before the coronation of England's Queen Elizabeth in 1953, Sir Edmund Hillary, along with his Sherpa guide Tenzing Norgay, became the first to reach the top of Mount Everest. Mountain adventures captivate me. I marvel at Jon Krakauer's account of the Himalayan catastrophe that claimed nine lives in one day in the spring of 1996. I am mesmerized by Moses' glowing adventures on Sinai and Abraham's sacrifice on Moriah. Even the tale of Much-Afraid who found hind's feet on high places thrills me.

Some climbed for the physical challenge, others to meet God, but they all heard a call: "Come up higher. There's more." More breathtaking panoramas. More simplicity. More clarity. More satisfaction at the summit. And more cost. Some mountain climbers lose their lives in the attempt.

For those who scale spiritual peaks, loss is certain—loss of life as we know it. All who scale these heights lose their lives because mountains of God's calling are known to humble even the greatest.

You have been at the feast and you have trained for the marathon. Your spirit is being set free. Your entanglements and expectations are being touched by the living God, but this adventure continues and God ups the ante. God is calling you higher. Why? Because that is where He is. Micah 4:2 says: "Come, let us go up to the mountain of the LORD, to the house of the God of Jacob."

Climbers anticipate four stages in any mountain adventure. They include the preparation, the way to and up the mountain, reaching the peak, and coming down. Allow me to share about these phases from Moses' encounter with the heights.

The Preparation

Anyone can climb a mountain. It is not gender specific. It does not require perfection in spiritual or physical fitness— although the better conditioned the climber is, the higher he or she can go. Still, the main requirement is formidable resolve. In his monumental *Into Thin Air* (Anchor, 1997), Krakauer says that it is "a triumph of desire over sensibility." In a spiritual climb you must set both your heart and your mind on the things above where Christ is (see Colossians 3:1–4).

Training is on the agenda of every climber. "Train yourself to be godly," Paul says. "For physical training is of some value, but godliness has value for all things, holding promise for both the present life and the life to come" (1 Timothy 4:7–8).

So how is it that God trains us? Mountain climbers pore over maps of slopes, glaciers, crevices and ravines. They carefully study the treks of those who have gone before. They talk to people who have been there. And they realize at least two things.

First, there must be a sure and steady call. Too much is at stake. Some force, bigger than self, must woo and enable. It has been said that "unless there is within us that which is above us, we will soon yield to that which is about us." And if it is about us, we will not scale any peak. Second, climbers know that any mountain will make a person feel small. This is true in both the physical and spiritual realms. You must know that it is God who wants you to come up higher and that it is an all-or-nothing proposition. You "can do everything through him who gives [you] strength" (Philippians 4:13). And "apart from [Him] you can do nothing" (John 15:5).

Moses knew the certainty of the call. It has been said that the book of Exodus chronicles two events: God taking the Israelites out of Egypt and God taking Egypt out of the Israelites. Chapter 19 is the hinge, the halfway point of the forty chapters, and there is a curious verse in this chapter: "The LORD descended to the top of Mount Sinai and called Moses to the top of the mountain. So Moses went up" (verse 20).

Did you get that? It says: "The LORD descended ... to the top." Nobody descends to the top. Not unless you are God. Moses knew that God wanted him on the heights with Him. How did he know? Because God descended to the highest point Moses could achieve and then called him up. How could Moses say no? How could I say no? How could you say no?

One of my favorite paintings is the "Creation of Adam." This masterpiece depicts two hands—of God and Adam—reaching toward one another. The fingers almost touch.

Almost, but not quite. Apologist Ravi Zacharias states in *Cries of the Heart* (Word, 1998):

> When you notice Michelangelo's painting of God reaching out to Adam, you see how outstretched God's arm is. Every muscle on His face is contorted, and the hand is reaching as far as possible to make contact. By contrast, Adam lackadaisically lets a limpish hand dangle with apathy in an attitude that seems to say, "If it meets it meets." That reflects the contrasting inclinations of the heart very well.

This Michelangelo fresco affirms that God descends, reaches and calls us up. Consider David's testimony: "You give me your shield of victory; you stoop down to make me great" (2 Samuel 22:36). A God who stoops is quite a picture. In Psalm 18:16, David adds: "He reached down from on high and took hold of me." In Exodus 3:8 God speaks: "I have come down . . . to bring them up."

God took hold of Moses and he was humbled. One cannot continue any mountain adventure without humility and brokenness. In *The Safest Place on Earth* (Word, 1999), noted Christian psychologist Larry Crabb says: "Brokenness is the realization that life is too much for us, not just because there is too much pain but also because we're too selfish. Brokenness is realizing He is all we have. Hope is realizing He is all we need. Joy is realizing He is all we want."

> For this is what the high and lofty One says—he who lives forever, whose name is holy: "I live in a high and holy place, but also with him who is contrite and lowly in spirit, to revive the spirit of the lowly and to revive the heart of the contrite."
>
> Isaiah 57:15

Moses is an apt role model for mountain climbing because in Numbers 12:3 he is called "a very humble man, more humble than anyone else on the face of the earth."

The stark contrast between the lavish Egyptian culture and the arid desert of Midian sparked Moses' metamorphosis; humility was the result. Moses changed from being an intimidator, one known as "powerful in speech and action" (Acts 7:22), to the timid one who confessed, "I have never been eloquent. . . . I am slow of speech and tongue" (Exodus 4:10). The self-assured Moses who had been "educated in all the wisdom of the Egyptians" (Acts 7:22) was the same man who begged "O Lord, please send someone else to [lead the Israelites out of Egypt]" (Exodus 4:13).

The man impatient with an Egyptian taskmaster was forbearing with the grumblings of thousands of Israelites. The self-indulgent Moses, accustomed to the servants and treasures of Pharaoh, became the forgiving one who was happy to be distinguished from all others just because God was with him (see Exodus 33:15–16). Critical Moses with the short fuse became Moses the intercessor. He sought God's healing for his foolishly strident sister, Miriam (see Numbers 12:9–13) and labored in prayer on behalf of the disobedient Hebrew multitude: "Now, please forgive their sin—but if not, then blot me out of the book you have written" (Exodus 32:32).

The pampered man who had everything to live for in the world's eyes was the one who gave it all up to see his God on the mountain. Hebrews 11:26 resounds: "He [Moses] regarded disgrace for the sake of Christ as of greater value than the treasures of Egypt, because he was looking ahead to his reward."

Acts 7:25 tells that "Moses thought that his own people would realize that God was using him to rescue them, but they did not." Moses was humbled. Moses saw the holy God revealed in a bush that did not burn up and it changed his life forever. He took off his sandals because he stood on holy ground. He knew his place and it was one of humility and brokenness. Now God could finally use him.

As the world sees it, changes should go in the opposite direction. A timid man should become forceful. A poor man depending on another for food should become self-sufficient. The world would send Moses to aggressiveness training or a positive thinking seminar or employ the latest success formula or push laws for leadership. But God's ways are different. Preparation for the mountain of God requires a humble heart. Are you up for that challenge?

Pride to humility and, with it, a fresh revelation of God. Moses was eighty years old when he leaned on God. He was hungry for Him and ready to lead others to the mountain.

The Way To and Up the Mountain

Most mountain climbers wonder what it is like at the apex and spend hours dreaming of adventures in the thin air. But that soon gives way, with glances in the direction of the distant summit, to sheer dread and nervous anticipation. There is reverence for the top. Awe. Though the climb lures like a siren, most of us get no further than base camp.

Moses led a ragtag expedition of people who saw only the value of being freed from their bondage. They never dreamed of being freed for the mountain of God. As they left Egypt with plunder aplenty, they found themselves in no fewer than forty wilderness campsites on the way to meet with God. They were in some places for months and some for days, depending on when the pillars of cloud and fire moved.

We will look briefly at seven of those campsites. Two things are true: God loves you wherever you are in the journey, and you may be in different places with differing roles at the same time. You may be, for instance, a certain distance from the peak with regard to each person who is important to you—spouse, parents, closest friends, children—and another distance in regard to your work, your church, your neighborhood or whatever affects your life. Here are the campsites:

1. Leaving Rameses (Exodus 12:31–42)

This is the place where freedom begins. Perhaps it is where you are. Rameses still echoed with the Egyptian cries of those mourning the deaths of their firstborn. As the Israelites left Egypt it was not hard to see the contrast between death and life, old ways and new, emptiness and backs that ached under the weight of the plunder God provided. Liberty is a reality.

You realize that His banner over you is love. You are unencumbered from your entanglements and your spirit is being set free. Like the children of Israel, your years of bondage are over and you are beginning your sojourn. But you need to travel swiftly. Move. Don't hesitate. Take the steps needed to go closer to the mountain.

2. On the Edge of the Desert (Exodus 13:20)

This campsite was called Etham, and it was their last stop before entering the vast expanse of desert. What was required there was courage. Can you imagine it? After centuries of hard labor, the Israelites were really rescued. But can you fathom the fear of leaving the familiar, though unhealthy, for the unknown? It took courage to walk the new walk toward the mountain of God.

It requires courage for you, too. Are you finding it difficult to take the step into the desert of the unknown? You know God has been setting you free, but the familiar has a tug that will not release you easily. You cannot move ahead if you will not take that first step over the edge onto hot sand. The best thing about it is that God is with you.

3. At the Sea (Exodus 14:2)

Pi Hahiroth. That was the dot on the map where the Israelites staked their tent pegs this time. It was here they realized that they had nowhere else to go but forward. They faced a sea ahead and an enemy army behind. What they needed was to face their fears and look for God's power. And what power! The waters parted and Moses and Miriam composed this song: "Who among the gods is like you, O LORD? Who is like you—majestic in holiness, awesome in glory, working wonders?" (Exodus 15:11).

What sea are you camped at? Who is like your God? How majestic is His holiness in your life? How awesome is His glory? What wonders is He working? What miracles will you look to Him for?

4. Near the Springs (Exodus 15:27)

The record states: "Then they came to Elim, where there were twelve springs and seventy palm trees, and they camped there near the water." It sounds like paradise. This was a place of blessing.

Are you at a place of blessing? Then beware, because blessing can lull us into apathy and superficiality. In *The Pressure's Off*, Larry Crabb says:

> If life presents only a few bumps, especially if they're small, I don't particularly care whether I know Christ well or not. I figure He's doing His job of blessing me and I'm doing my job of living responsibly. Rather than a thirsty deer panting after water, I'm more like a hibernating bear with paws resting on my full stomach.

To get to the top of the mountain you must not allow the pleasantness of God's blessing to keep you at a comfortable place. I challenge you to seek not just His hands but His face. To see His glory better, you will need to climb the mountain.

5. At a Place with No Water (Exodus 17:1)

As wonderful as the previous campsite had been, this one was the pits. At Rephidim they experienced thirst and began grumbling. This is where the Israelites complained, "Is the LORD among us or not?" (Exodus 17:7). It is where Moses got so frustrated with the people that he struck the rock inappropriately and reaped God's displeasure (see Numbers 20:8–13). It is where enemy attacks from the Amalekites came against them. It is where Aaron and Hur held up Moses' arms and the opposition was defeated. At this campsite, unity was needed.

Are you at a thirsty place? Are you grumbling and quarreling, maybe even with God's appointed leaders? Or maybe you are the leader. Are you frustrated? Have you entertained the thought, *Is God with me or not?* Are you under attack? Find those who will hold up your arms so you can move into victory. The mountain is just around the corner.

6. Near the Mountain (Exodus 18:5)

You can see the mountain in the distance. Your adrenaline rushes. Your heart pounds. This is a place for listening to wise counsel, just as Moses did when his father-in-law, Jethro, reminded him of the art of delegating responsibility. Perseverance is needed. Don't give up now.

7. In Front of the Mountain (Exodus 19:2)

No longer was Mount Sinai a figment of their imagination. This was the real thing; the bona fide, scary thing. The time had arrived.

Exodus 19:16 captures the pathos of base camp: "On the morning of the third day there was thunder and lightning, with a thick cloud over the mountain, and a very loud trumpet blast. Everyone in the camp trembled." I bet they did. God had told them they were not to go up the mountain until the trumpet blared and now they heard it. Do you hear it? The shofar is blowing. God is summoning His people into His presence.

> Then Moses led the people out of the camp to meet with God, and they stood at the foot of the mountain. Mount Sinai was covered with smoke, because the LORD descended on it in fire. The smoke billowed up from it like smoke from a furnace, the whole mountain trembled violently, and the sound of the trumpet grew louder and louder. Then Moses spoke and the voice of God answered him.
>
> Exodus 19:17–19

The Lord is calling. The trumpet's decibels are rising. "Come up higher. There's more." On the summit you can see His glory. You can hear Him proclaim His name. And you can bow down.

At the Summit

The summit casts an awesome spell on our souls. God lures us into His presence and one little glimpse forever calls us higher. It is there we can see the Holy One. It is there that our own unholiness is revealed. It is there that our reasoning pales next to His wisdom. This is similar to the way the physical mind becomes inept in the oxygen-deprived air at the peak. But we were meant for other worlds, higher places. Paul told the Philippians that God had "called [him] heavenward in Christ Jesus" (Philippians 3:14). Not earthward.

So much of our lives is lived on lower plateaus or even in dark valleys. When we are broken and humbled, we begin to see the view from the top. We expect that brokenness will cast us downward, but, just as God promised, as we humble ourselves, He lifts us up (see 1 Peter 5:6). Vistas, hidden before, are now plain. I believe, also, that the summit is where we begin to see the longings not just of our hearts, but of God's heart. We begin to see something of the vast panorama that He sees. And when we come alongside God in His desires, our own longings are met far beyond imagination.

These are the words the Lord called out to Moses on the heights:

> Tell the people of Israel: "You yourselves have seen what I did to Egypt, and how I carried you on eagles' wings and brought you to myself. Now if you obey me fully and keep my covenant, then out of all nations you will be my treasured possession. Although the whole earth is mine, you will be for me a kingdom of priests and a holy nation."
>
> Exodus 19:4–6

Eagles in Scripture symbolize freedom and the phrase that follows it tells why God gave us liberty: "I brought you to myself." The great God who reaches toward us, who stoops, who takes the initiative, longs to be connected with us. Then He says, "You will be my treasured possession." He works painstakingly at convincing us that we are His cherished ones.

Then God says, "You will be for me a kingdom of priests." Jack Hayford, in *Worship His Majesty* (Regal, 2000), offers an important insight about priests: "*Pontifex* is the Latin word for priest. The real meaning lies in the original meaning of 'pontifex': 'bridge builder.' Priesthood was always meant to be something practical—to help us cross over, or to get from here to there." Paul calls it being "Christ's ambassadors" with a "ministry of reconciliation" (see 2 Corinthians 5:18–20). And as if that was not enough, God says He wants us to be "a holy nation."

In this one Scripture, we see five of God's "heart longings" for us: (1) freedom; (2) connection; (3) treasure; (4) priesthood; and (5) holiness.

Why are these His longings?

He wants our spirits free so we can worship Him. Do you remember God's words to Pharaoh through Moses? "Let my people go, so that they may worship me" (see Exodus 4:23; 5:1; 7:16; 8:1, 20; 9:1, 13; 10:3). He did not say, "Let My people go, so that they may work for Me." He was rescuing them from the stronghold of slavedrivers.

Why connection? Jesus explained in His High Priestly prayer: "Father, I want those you have given me to be with me where I am" (John 17:24).

Why convince us we are treasured? It is because we are the pinnacle of His creation, "made . . . a little lower than the heavenly beings and crowned . . . with glory and honor" (Psalm 8:5). What a majestic, mysterious God!

Why make us a bridge through priesthood? "To let the world know that you [the Father] sent me [the Son] and have loved them even as you have loved me" (John 17:23).

And why does He want us to live holy lives? It is because "without holiness no one will see the Lord" (Hebrews 12:14).

Like Isaiah, God wants us to see Him at the top, "high and exalted" (see Isaiah 6:1–8). He longs for us to hear Him and feel Him and smell the sweet aroma of Jesus in every place. He wants us to taste Him. He wants all our senses alive, worshiping. Why? Because His glory is revealed.

Moses understood this. His humbling in the desert gave him freedom to see God's glory. He was connected with God. God said:

> "When a prophet of the Lord is among you, I reveal myself to him in visions, I speak to him in dreams. But this is not true of my servant Moses; he is faithful in all my house. With him I speak face to face, clearly and not in riddles; he sees the form of the Lord."
>
> Numbers 12:6–8

Moses knew he was treasured by God and so were the people he led in the wilderness. For forty years their clothes and sandals did not wear out. Moses was a priest. He spoke to God on behalf of the people and he uttered the words of the Lord to the people. That is quite a bridge. And Moses lived in holiness. I know, because he saw God.

Are you living God's longings or are you simply resting among your blessings like that hibernating bear mentioned earlier? Think about it. Is your spirit free? Free enough to worship Him before you work for Him? Are you connected with Him or are you withholding from Him? Do you know you are His treasure—polished, showcased and protected?

Are you a priest, a bridge, someone He could make His appeal through? (See 2 Corinthians 5:20.) And what is your holiness quotient? Your HQ? Does He need to purge and purify you?

Coming Down

Jon Krakauer says that "the summit [is] really only the halfway point."

Moses did not know the art of rappelling off a mountain, but this contemporary way down is instructive for us. When a climber rappels down, he or she uses ropes to bounce off the face of the mountain backward; one's eyes naturally look up. The only other option is to go down face forward, looking into the valley below. With that latter choice of descent, we just might fall and smash our faces on the rocks.

It is a matter of focus. We need to be aware of the valley, and the people waiting there, but our eyes need to be turned toward the heights. It is this looking up posture that keeps us depending on "him who is able to keep [us] from falling and to present [us] before his glorious presence" (Jude 24). It is the stance of one who is humble.

We have to come down. It is not at the peak that we live out God's longings. We become aware of them at the summit, but we put them into action below. It is only when we live in community below that we understand God's heart. It is about Him. It is His renown that matters. We can get a shiny face, like Moses, on top of the mountain, but we reflect God's glory in the valley where darkness lurks. But how do we do it?

In the retelling of his testimony before King Agrippa, the apostle Paul gives us a blueprint. These are the words Jesus spoke to him on the road to Damascus.

"Now get up and stand on your feet. I have appeared to you to appoint you as a servant and as a witness of what you have seen of me and what I will show you. I will rescue you from your own people and from the Gentiles. I am sending you to them to open their eyes and turn them from darkness to light, and from the power of Satan to God, so that they may receive forgiveness of sins and a place among those who are sanctified by faith in me."

Acts 26:16–18

Follow as we look at the verses backward. First, from verse 26:18, God offers two gifts: forgiveness and a place to belong. Christian psychologists note that these are mankind's most crucial longings. We cannot give them away, but we can introduce others to Christ who has the power to offer them.

Next we are told what God wants us to do when we come off the summit. The answer is threefold: Open the eyes of those around us, turn them from darkness to light and turn them from the power of Satan to God. Once again, we cannot do that, but we can offer Jesus who does have the power to accomplish the task.

Third, we learn that this job is not easy. If we have to be "rescued" from the people we go to, we can count on the return not being a cakewalk. Paul explains why this is true in an idolatrous culture: "There is but one God, the Father, from whom all things came and for whom we live; and there is but one Lord, Jesus Christ, through whom all things came and through whom we live. But not everyone knows this" (1 Corinthians 8:6–7). Jesus makes it clear: "In this world you will have trouble. But take heart! I have overcome the world" (John 16:33).

The fourth insight is the key to it all. Acts 26:16 gives us two titles and neither is lofty. God says when we come off the mountain He wants us to be servants and witnesses. He does not say that He wants us to be lords of the manor—He is asking us to be servants. His desire is not that we be judges, prosecutors or even defense lawyers. He wants witnesses, people who will tell with accuracy what they have seen of Him and what He will show them in the future. That means that we have to stay close. Anybody can be a servant and a witness—anybody who is willing to be humble.

Verse 16 tells us how to start: We are to get up and stand on our feet. We are to start making our way down the mountain. But remember this: Someone once said that we are never as tall as when we kneel to pray. This job will not get done without lots of intercession.

And, last, the first word of the passage tells us when we are to do this: Now.

It's About Time

The only psalm on record by Moses is Psalm 90. In these words he makes it clear that we are finite and God is infinite. We are bound by time. God is not. Our time on earth will inevitably involve some troubling circumstances, and He cares how we use it. That is why in Psalm 90:12 Moses' prayer is: "Teach us to number our days, that we may present to You a heart of wisdom" (NASB). We can either waste time, spend time living in a rut or invest time. Wise investments happen when we use resources now for something that will outlast those assets. There are only three eternal things: God, His Word and His people. On the summit, things become simpler and we can bring that clarity down to earth. Then we don't just count days; we make them count.

Mountain climbing is all about time. It starts with intense preparations days, weeks, months ahead. Once on the climb, scaling rocks or ice is a slow and meticulous process. Trying to suck in the air at the summit saps precious strength. And rappelling down carelessly and quickly means certain disaster.

Someone has once said that if you want to know the value of one year, ask a family with a child who failed a grade. If you want to know the value of one month, ask a mother who just delivered a premature baby. If you want to know the value of one week, ask a weekly newspaper editor. If you want to understand the value of one hour, ask two lovers longing to meet. If you want to know the value of one minute, ask someone who just missed the train. If you want to know the value of one second, ask a driver who narrowly avoided an accident. And if you want to know the value of one millisecond, ask a silver medalist in the Olympics.

Moses lived 120 years. According to Moses himself that is more than an average lifespan: "The length of our days is seventy years—or eighty, if we have the strength; yet their span is but trouble and sorrow, for they quickly pass, and we fly away" (Psalm 90:10).

But Moses predicts contentment for the people of God as we live out our days. He asks God to "satisfy us in the morning with your unfailing love, that we may sing for joy and be glad all our days" (verse 14). Moses learned to pray that way on the summit. I think we can trust his judgment.

Does the mountain of God entice your heart? I encourage you to ascend to the highest point you can reach. Ask the God who descends to the top to help you.

And then turn with me to the story of Abraham, who found not glory, but sacrifice, on his mountain.

Searching for More

1. Where do you think you are right now in your spiritual journey: In humbling preparation for the peak? On the way to the mountain? Climbing? At the summit? Rappelling down?

2. Of the longings of God's heart we discussed, which is hardest for you to embrace? Which is easiest? Why?

___ Freedom ___ Connection ___ Treasure
___ Priesthood ___ Holiness

3. What are you seeing of God that you can tell others about?

8

Sacrifice on the Mountain

*W*illiam Shakespeare penned these famous words: "All the world's a stage, and all the men and women merely players: they have their exits and their entrances, and one man in his time plays many parts."

Think about the many parts you play, or, in today's parlance, the many "hats" women wear—daughter, granddaughter, in-law, sister, wife, friend, mother, church member, neighbor. You may add "hats" of giftedness to this list of relationships. You may be a pianist or cellist, a soloist, speaker, writer, Bible teacher, scholar. Perhaps some of the baggage from the past identifies you as well. You may be the product of a dysfunctional home or a victim of incest or rape. You may even be wearing a hat assigned to you by the opinions and words of others. Perhaps they have given you a dunce's cap. Yes, we all play many parts and these are what make up identities.

The word *identity* has gotten great attention of late. There is identity theft and identity crises, for example. Identity is like a shadow. It follows us around, but until it is purified by God's hand, we will never know what it is that He intends for us to be. Without His opinion, we somehow shrink and become smaller than intended. His plan for us is the only one that matters. Our real identity comes in the destiny He assigns to us. It is not our possessions or position or popularity, or lack thereof, that determines who we really are. It is not the opinions or expectations of others. It is not so much what we do as who we are—or, perhaps, *whose* we are—that determines our identity.

Abraham understood this and his mountain adventure caused him to surrender what he thought was his identity for something even better. Mount Sinai brought Moses an encounter with the glory of God; Mount Moriah brought Abraham face-to-face with the God who requires sacrifice.

Have you determined what hats you wear, what things make up your identity? Then would you consider climbing Mount Moriah with me and bringing to God a sacrifice?

Finding True Identity

Abraham was given his identity by God through words and a covenant. Abraham saw himself as a man of the tent. And he was a man who built altars. But God told him he was to be "a father of many nations" (Genesis 17:5). How absurd this must have seemed! Abraham had no children, so the concept of fatherhood was foreign to him. But, nonetheless, that was the identity God revealed. I wonder if God has an identity for you that you think is ridiculous.

I remember well when my college speech professor spoke these words to me: "I will give you a *C* for this course, but, count on it, you don't have what it takes to be a public speaker." For years I assumed that my fate had been sealed, but God had other plans. I have been a national women's retreat speaker since 1980. What seemed absurd in the early years became a new, wonderful identity in later years. Why? Because God touched it.

You no doubt recall that when God promised a son to Abraham and his wife, Sarah, she actually laughed at the prospect because they were far past childbearing years. I still marvel every time I read Paul's words declaring this patriarch's faith in God's promise.

> Against all hope, Abraham in hope believed and so became the father of many nations, just as it had been said to him, "So shall your offspring be." Without weakening in his faith, he faced the fact that his body was as good as dead—since he was about a hundred years old—and that Sarah's womb was also dead. Yet he did not waver through unbelief regarding the promise of God, but was strengthened in his faith and gave glory to God, being fully persuaded that God had power to do what he had promised.
>
> Romans 4:18–21

In time, God did do what He had promised. Isaac was born. You also know, of course, of the costly shortcut Abraham and Sarah took with her maidservant Hagar. Ishmael was born before Isaac because they had a hard time waiting for the identity God had intended. But Ishmael was not the child of the promise. Isaac was the beginning of the celestial tally. Remember, Genesis 15:5 describes how God took Abraham outside and said, "'Look up at the heavens and count the stars—if indeed you can count them.' Then he said to him, 'So shall your offspring be.'"

That little bit of history is important because now we move to another faith chapter in Abraham's life. His chronicle as a mountain climber began in Genesis 22:2 when God said, "Take your son, your only son, Isaac, whom you love, and go to the region of Moriah. Sacrifice him there as a burnt offering on one of the mountains I will tell you about."

This could seem confusing. God had told Abraham his identity was in being a father, yet here He told him to kill the child of promise. Make no mistake: God was also demanding Abraham sacrifice his very identity. God wanted to know if He was more important than all else. It is one of the things that happens on the mountain. We are forever altered. But if we are obedient, as Abraham was, the result is amazing. God provides and intimacy occurs. I believe the best biblical definition of intimacy comes from this passage of Scripture, words that God spoke to Abraham as he picked up the knife to slay his bound son: "Do not do anything to him. Now I know that you fear God, because you have not withheld from me your son, your only son" (Genesis 22:12). Intimacy means nothing held back.

This is another place that requires an open hand. When we surrender our identities, His identity shines forth and we prove that our desire is truly His name and renown, not our own. Martin Luther is credited with saying, "I have held many things in my hands, and I have lost them all; but whatever I have placed in God's hands, that I still possess."

No one can take from us what we have already offered up. If your identity is in your children, then an empty nest is devastating. If your identity is in your job, then a layoff will do you in. If applause is your identity, then silence will diminish you. But if He is your identity—your life—then it is gain whether you live or die, own much or are destitute, have children or are barren, are noticed or ignored. Paul said, "For to me, to live is Christ and to die is gain" (Philippians 1:21).

Even mature Christians struggle here. I met recently with a woman who heads a highly respected national ministry. She said she could not get Philippians 1:21 off her mind and heart. She confessed, "For me to live is Christ. And my husband, and my ministry, and my speaking, and my travels. But I am squaring off with cancer and if anything but Christ is my life, then to die is not gain."

Generally two groups of people have the hardest time surrendering their identities to God. The first group is composed of those who have just come to Christ, because they are still figuring out their identities. The second group is more complicated. They are the ones who have walked with God for a long time and appear to have it all together. They try to defend their images, sometimes unknowingly. But God is looking for broken, contrite, humbled, surrendered hearts. He longs for people to be just as He wants them to be, not as they suppose they should be or as others are. The mountain is part of God's plan to see this process through to completion.

Hasidic tradition tells a story of a rabbi named Zusya. It seems the learned one died and went to stand before God at the Judgment. He waited for the Judge. He wrung his hands. He furrowed his brow. He convinced himself that God would ask, "Why were you not more like Abraham or Moses or David?" But, when God arrived, He simply asked, "Why were you not more like Zusya?"

To help us become all that He intends, God will sometimes test us. Genesis 22:1 says: "Some time later God tested Abraham." You can bet it came at just the right time. We find evidence of God's testing throughout Scripture, and His motive is different in each situation. But generally He seems to be observing what is in a person's heart or watching to see if the people will listen and obey. God's testing also leads to humbling so that, in the end, it might go well for the people. And, always, it reveals whether or not the called ones "fear God"—that is, love Him with all their hearts and souls.

God will test us but He will never tempt us. Satan is the author of temptation. That is why God makes this promise in 1 Corinthians 10:13:

> No temptation has seized you except what is common to man. And God is faithful; he will not let you be tempted beyond what you can bear. But when you are tempted, he will also provide a way out so that you can stand up under it.

Contrast that word with Paul's testimony in 2 Corinthians 1:8–9:

> We do not want you to be uninformed, brothers, about the hardships we suffered in the province of Asia. We were under great pressure, far beyond our ability to endure, so that we despaired even of life. Indeed, in our hearts we felt the sentence of death. But this happened that we might not rely on ourselves but on God, who raises the dead.

Abraham probably felt great pressure. It is true that God will not allow us to be tempted beyond what we can bear. But He will allow more testing than we think we can endure. "You want me to kill my son?" Abraham may have said. But God tested him and used the situation so that Abraham might not rely on himself, but on the God powerful enough to raise the dead.

And He may want to test you at the mountain as well. Testing that draws us higher to the divine can only come from the hand of God. When our surrender results, intimacy with Him happens. Undaunted, Abraham responded immediately. Genesis 22:3 says: "Early the next morning Abraham got up and saddled his donkey." That would be like setting your alarm clock in order to get up early to do the unthinkable. Like revving the engine on your Ford Explorer to race to the peak where everything you hold dearest will be given away. But Abraham cut the wood and set out. Let's follow his trek up the mountain.

Fixing Our Eyes on God

Several phrases in the account in Genesis 22:1–19 show the progression of the test of Abraham's true identity. They help us understand how Abraham could keep his eyes on God during this difficult journey.

1. God referred to Isaac as "your son, your only son . . . whom you love" (Genesis 22:2; see also verses 12, 16).

Three times in the story this phrase "your son, your only son" is used. It spurs us to think of several New Testament verses:

- "For God so loved the world that he gave his one and only Son, that whoever believes in him shall not perish but have eternal life" (John 3:16).
- "A voice from heaven said, 'This is my Son, whom I love; with him I am well pleased'" (Matthew 3:17).

127

- "He himself bore our sins in his body on the tree, so that we might die to sins and live for righteousness; by his wounds you have been healed" (1 Peter 2:24).

Abraham sacrificed Isaac. It was a prefiguring of the ultimate sacrifice the Father made of His Son, His only Son whom He loved, on Mount Calvary for our benefit. Surrender is requested on your mountain, but God is not asking you to do anything He has not already done. What a privilege for us to follow His example!

2. *"Abraham looked up and saw the place [of sacrifice] in the distance.... Abraham looked up and there in a thicket he saw a ram" (Genesis 22:4, 13).*

When Abraham looked up he saw where God wanted his identity slain and later he saw God's provision in the midst of it all. That makes me think of the words God told Ezekiel to speak in the valley of dry bones: "Come from the four winds, O breath, and breathe into these slain, that they may live" (Ezekiel 37:9). God knows what needs to be slain and the Holy Spirit sees to it that what is surrendered to Him and willingly put to death brings life in the end.

Abraham did not see until he looked. And he did not fix his gaze on a horizontal target. He looked up. His direction did not come from man and neither did his help. How did Abraham know to look up? Remember, when God initially offered the covenant He took Abraham outside and said, "Look up at the heavens ..." (Genesis 15:5). Do you look up? Or do you look horizontally to people for your guidance and aid?

*3. Abraham said to the servants with him, "We [Isaac
and I] will worship and then we will come back to
you" (Genesis 22:5).*

Isn't it interesting that the label Abraham gave this encounter with God on Mount Moriah was . . . worship? The
handing over of what he longed for and loved the most was
called . . . worship. Tai Anderson of the Christian recording
group Third Day is credited with saying: "If [worship] is
just an experience, then it only lasts for a few hours. But if
it's an offering, it lasts your whole life."

And did you notice Abraham's choice of words in the
last part of that phrase? He said, "We will worship and
then we will come back." We. What faith in the provision
of His God! Three times in the faith chapter, Hebrews 11,
it is said of this patriarch: "By faith Abraham. . . ." Oh, for
that to be true of me and you!

*4. "[Abraham] himself carried the fire and the knife"
(Genesis 22:6).*

Of all the phrases that are curious in this passage, I find
this one to be the most intriguing. Surely Abraham needed
fire to burn the offering and he required a knife to slay his
son. But there is more to it. If any revelation is to happen
on any mountain where we meet God, it will come because
both the Holy Spirit and the Word of God partner for us
to see it.

Using the image of fire in relation to the work of the
Holy Spirit is not a new thing. When Elijah battled the
priests of Baal on another mountain, we are told "the fire of
the Lord fell" and the result was that the people saw it, fell
down and cried, "The LORD—he is God! The LORD—he is
God!" (1 Kings 18:39). Moses saw Mt. Sinai covered with

smoke "because the LORD descended on it in fire" (Exodus 19:18).

When David built an altar on Araunah's threshing floor, "the LORD answered him with fire from heaven on the altar of burnt offering" (1 Chronicles 21:26). By the way, that is the very site where Abraham had laid Isaac on the altar of sacrifice and the place where Solomon's Temple was eventually built (see 2 Samuel 24 and 2 Chronicles 3:1). In Acts 2:3–4 we read that God filled the disciples with the Holy Spirit on Pentecost, and the people "saw what seemed to be tongues of fire that separated and came to rest on each of them."

It is also noteworthy that the Word of God is revealed as a knife. Hebrews 4:12 says: "For the word of God is living and active. Sharper than any double-edged sword, it penetrates even to dividing soul and spirit, joints and marrow; it judges the thoughts and attitudes of the heart." In Revelation 1:16, this vision is given of Jesus: "Out of his mouth came a sharp double-edged sword." Ephesians 6:17 teaches that the one offensive piece of the armor of God is called "the sword of the Spirit, which is the word of God."

The Holy Spirit and the Word of God. Fire and sword. This is the way we receive revelations from God.

Do you allow both to operate in your life?

5. *"When they reached the place . . . , Abraham built an altar there and arranged the wood on it"* (*Genesis 22:9*).

Abraham's sacrifice was imminent, but before he raised the knife in obedience, he lingered at a familiar place. He built an altar and tarried to arrange the wood. Do you give in to the familiar and the religious on your way to obedience?

6. *"I will surely bless you" (Genesis 22:17)*.

Job and Mary and the Prodigal, the paralytic, Naaman and Moses. All discovered that the end was better than the beginning. When God first revealed the covenant to Abraham He told him to count the stars: "So shall your offspring be" (Genesis 15:5). But when Abraham surrendered Isaac, God made an addition to this declaration: "I will surely bless you and make your descendants as numerous as the stars in the sky and as the sand on the seashore" (Genesis 22:17).

With God, the return never ends. You cannot out-give Him. Abraham received much for his obedience. Intimacy. Revelation. Blessing. "All nations on earth will be blessed, because you have obeyed me" (Genesis 22:18). How has God out-given you?

7. *"Abraham stayed in Beersheba" (Genesis 22:19)*.

When Abraham returned to his servants, just as he had promised, they all left together for Beersheba. That is significant because Beersheba was where they started from. But now they were returning as transformed people. For one thing, they understood the fear of the Lord. In *The Message*, Eugene Peterson says it this way: "Now I know how fearlessly you fear God" (Genesis 22:12). They would forever take God seriously, and obey.

Tracing Abraham's Steps

What would it look like if you went back to the place you had been before a transforming work of God? How would it appear to your family? How about your friends, neighbors and work associates? What about those at church?

If you climbed Abraham's mountain and surrendered your identity and God really had the most important place in your life, what would it look like? I suspect your home would be overflowing with Him, a hundredfold return for opening your hands. Your family life would be more about holiness than about happiness. Your church would be a place of worship first and work second. Your ministry would contain no hype and manipulation; just Him. Your workplace would be about His glory, not what you can get. Your neighborhood would be filled with light, not lust. No desperate housewives on your block.

It would be like Isaiah 32:2: "Each man [and woman] will be like a shelter from the wind and a refuge from the storm, like streams of water in the desert and the shadow of a great rock in a thirsty land."

My experience says it is so: God has asked for surrender in every part of the list that makes up my identity, but surrender always results in the assurance that God is faithful. Let me give you an example. It is possible that the hardest area for me to surrender has involved my identity as a mother—affected, I presume, by the fact that two of my children are insulin-dependent diabetics. Yet He has clearly directed me to stop defending my image, humble myself and allow my children, now adults, to help me become all that He intended.

Our youngest son, Mark, was seven when he received the diabetic diagnosis. Shortly after that difficult news, our whole family attended our church's Sweet Spirit Party—an alternative to Halloween. Everyone dressed in costumes that depicted either Bible verses or Bible characters. We played games, had refreshments and waited with anticipation for the premier event—the candy march.

The candy march was signaled by the playing of music. Parents stood in a big circle ready with stashes of sweets. Children formed a circle on the inside and, marching to the beat of the tunes, held open their sacks to receive goodies from the adults.

It hit me. "John, we have to go home."

"Why?"

"This is cruel. It's not fair to Mark to give him a whole bag of candy and then whisk it away. We have to leave. Mark will not be able to handle this."

My wise husband responded. "Is it Mark who can't handle it, or you?"

"Oh, no, it's definitely Mark."

"We're not going to leave, Marilyn."

"If you really loved me, you'd let us go home."

"We're not leaving. Mark needs to know that life without sugar is just as sweet as life with sugar."

Once my husband knows something is right, there is no moving him. We stayed. Mark joined the inner circle. He marched along and his sack grew full. Then he sat down on the floor of the fellowship hall and emptied out his treasure. And we saw that God's faithfulness was ever before us. The other parents, moved by God, had planned ahead. Some gave him pencils with his name on them. Some gave sugar-free candy. Some offered bags of pennies or books. Mark got more than all the other children. The sugar he got from people who did not know of his challenge, he gave away—happily.

If we had gone home that day, we would have missed the faithfulness of God. Surrender preceded that knowledge. More intimacy with God was the result. We remained in the church family and were transformed—actually, everyone's view of our amazing and gracious God was affected. He received praise and honor.

Another area in which I have found my identity is in my role as a Bible teacher. I have often needed to admit that I don't know very much; I cannot teach anybody anything. But I can bring people right in front of Jesus by His grace so He can do as He chooses. Even though I am an "ordinary" vessel, being in Jesus' presence makes me fit for His use (see Acts 4:13). Echoing the words of Peter and John to the crippled beggar (see Acts 3:6), in the name of Jesus I give the best I have to offer. That's true for all of us.

That Scripture, in turn, formed the basis for my identity as an author, and leads to the testimony of surrender regarding this book you now hold. The manuscript had been in flux for five years prior to its publication. I tried knocking on every door I could find—personal contacts, people who knew people, writer's conferences with acquisition editors. I even hired a book agent—a wonderful woman who worked hard for me.

But God kept pressing me to surrender the book to Him. I thought He was crazy. I was getting some of my identity from its pages so it was difficult to hold it with an open hand. One night, however, I dared to e-mail my book agent and tell her that it was time to pull the plug on the project that had been languishing at some publishing houses. I thought it was certain death for material I knew God had given me.

Just a day and a half later I was presenting a retreat in Annapolis, Maryland, when the editor responsible for getting this work into print approached me to discuss publication possibilities. The timing was unmistakable. I had opened my hands, offering my identity as a writer, and God blessed.

He gave me intimacy with Him, revelation of Him and . . . a book contract.

So where are you in your pilgrimage? Trace Abraham's steps once more:

- God asked Abraham to sacrifice his son. Did God nudge you to surrender some aspect of your identity as you read this chapter?
- Abraham made preparations to go where God told him to go. He cut the wood for the burnt offering and rose early. Are you going to obey or are you pursuing a shortcut?
- Abraham looked up and saw the place God ordained. Have you seen the place God told you about? Are you there?
- When Abraham reached the place, he built an altar and arranged the wood on it. Are you building familiar altars and religiously arranging wood?
- Abraham took the fire up the mountain and raised his knife over the sacrifice. Are the Spirit and the Word active in your life? Has God said, "On the mountain of the Lord, it will be provided"?
- For Abraham the end was better than the beginning. Are you enjoying intimacy, revelation and blessing?
- Abraham was transformed. Do you fearlessly fear God?

Sacrifice at the top is never easy, but Jesus' words encourage us to keep climbing the mountain: "And everyone who has left houses or brothers or sisters or father or mother or children or fields for my sake will receive a hundred times as much and will inherit eternal life" (Matthew 19:29).

Searching for More

1. What hats do you wear that form your identity?
2. Is there an identity that God has revealed for you that you think is absurd? What is it?
3. Do you more often look up to God for direction and help, or do you look out to others?
4. Describe a time that you allowed both the Word of God and the Holy Spirit of God to partner in bringing revelation of Him and His desires to your heart.
5. Tell about a time of surrender that brought you intimacy, revelation and blessing from God.
6. Where are you in the identity surrender journey?

    _____ Entertaining God's request
    _____ Preparing to obey
    _____ Seeing the place
    _____ At the place
    _____ Building altars and arranging wood
    _____ Knife raised
    _____ Seeing provision
    _____ Enjoying the blessing of it all

9

The Chosen Spot

Recently our family traveled to western Maryland to enjoy a Memorial Day weekend together. On the way, we encountered fog so thick on Big Savage Mountain we could not see six feet in front of us. The driver ahead slowed to a stop—on the interstate. Having nowhere to go, we rear-ended her SUV. Our bodily injuries were minor but our car was totaled. There were many accidents that day; one pileup several miles behind us involved 75 cars.

At that spot on the mountain, Jesus looked at us and we looked at Him. The sky had descended in dense fog but His message was clear. He seemed to say: "There are places in your life right now that seem to be in a fog. You can't even see an exit to get off. But if you stop, others will pile up behind you and get injured. So keep moving slowly ahead." In other words, *persevere.*

If God has been birthing desire in you, don't miss the spot of connection with the divine. It might be on a foggy mountain. It might be on a clear peak. Or, if you are not up to the challenge a mountain presents, maybe your connection point will be no higher than a treetop. It might be in a pleasant place or in a difficult place. But make no mistake. Jesus longs to meet you, and me, at the spot of His choice.

What kind of spot are you in at present? Have cancer cells challenged your body? Are financial reversals imminent? Or are you enjoying a new baby or maybe a first grandchild? Are you reveling in dreams come true? Or are there some nightmares? Is there a message from God burning in your heart that perhaps others have misunderstood? Are you seeing God at work in big ways?

We are all in some kind of spot, a place that God may have designed or allowed. It is a place where He looks at us, meets us and touches us in transforming ways. How gracious of God to go to so much trouble to engineer our being at the spot—the place of divine connection—just at the right moment!

That is what happened to a short man named Zacchaeus. His story is recorded in Luke 19:1–10. God had placed a desire in his heart to see who Jesus was, but because the crowd was large—and tall—he could not see Him. Did he give up? No. His desire forced him to run ahead and climb a sycamore-fig tree just to get a glimpse. And when he did, his life was changed forever.

Luke 19:5 says: "When Jesus reached the spot, he looked up and said to him, 'Zacchaeus, come down immediately. I must stay at your house today.'" In *The God Chasers* (Destiny, 1999), Tommy Tenney says that "it takes longer to grow a sycamore tree than it does to grow a man." He asserts: "The truth is that we have all 'come short of the glory of God' and cannot see him face-to-face without divine assistance."

Can you picture it? God the Father sits on the throne calculating the exact spots in our lives where we might connect with Him—not just at salvation, but all through our lives. His eyes sparkle as we get it and meet Him at exactly the right moment . . . just as He planned. Some people call these times "defining moments," and there are usually only a handful in each life.

Before we dissect Zacchaeus' tree climbing adventure, let's consider some thoughts about desire. Walter Brueggemann is credited with saying that "faith on its way to maturity moves from duty to delight." If Zacchaeus had been fulfilling a duty, he probably would have gone to the Temple. But delight caused him to run and climb a tree just to get a glimpse of Jesus. Duty is the opposite of desire and desire brings delight.

Duty is what finds you outlining a Bible passage according to a study formula. Delight is what drives the "aha moment" in one line of the text meant just for you. Duty is what makes you plod into your church board meeting. Delight is what motivates the times you can hardly stay seated because God is meeting you in church, and you want to jump up and down and clap your hands. Duty is what gets you to invite a neighbor to the evangelistic outreach program at your church. Delight is what happens when you cultivate an honest friendship, find out what is going on in your neighbor's life and giggle over coffee with her. Delight sprouts when you get to tell her about your Jesus, the One who enables you to meet each day with a smile no matter what is going on.

In his book *The Journey of Desire* (Nelson, 2000), John Eldredge says this:

> Not a symphony has been written, a mountain climbed, an injustice fought, or a love sustained apart from desire. Desire

fuels our search for the life we prize. Our desire, if we will listen to it, will save us from committing soul-suicide, the sacrifice of our hearts on the altar of "getting by." The same old thing is not enough. It never will be.

Zacchaeus operated on desire. Otherwise, why would he make it his business to know that Jesus would be passing by? Why would he run ahead? And why would he bag his pompous image to climb a tree? If he wanted more knowledge, he could have hung out with the Pharisees. Or he could have satisfied his desire with the purchase of another self-gratifying toy with the funds absconded from his tax collections.

My question is simple: What level of desire do you have to reach the top of a mountain, or even a tree, to get a glimpse of Jesus? And, maybe even more telling, what choices are you making that reduce your desire for Him? Perhaps you swap going to the heights with Him for things in your comfort level. Things like overeating. Purchasing too much. Drinking to excess. Praying to be seen by others. Memorizing verses with a competitive spirit. Attending countless seminars but never changing.

Again Eldredge reminds us:

> The Jews of the day were practicing a very soul-killing spirituality, a lifeless religion of duty and obligation. They had abandoned desire and replaced it with knowledge and performance as the key to life. The synagogue was the place to go to learn how to get with the program. Desire was out of the question; duty was the path that people must walk. No wonder they feared Jesus. He came along and started appealing to desire.

Are you more inclined to get with the program, or kick up your heels with glee at a sight of the Master?

Jesus' Approach

Answering the questions of a news reporter will help us understand Zacchaeus' situation. Where did this all happen? Luke 19:1 says: "Jesus entered Jericho and was passing through." The Lord was not intending to stay in Jericho. This is also the place where Tenney suggests the crowd planned for Palm Sunday began to gather steam. It started on the road outside Jericho where many watched as a blind man named Bartimaeus was healed. Then salvation came to Zacchaeus and his house, and the parade grew in numbers. By the time they reached Jerusalem, there were many in the crowd to wave palm branches and laud their hero.

Who were the principal characters in the story? Zacchaeus, the chief tax collector, is the primary player. Then there is the crowd. They were described as mutterers (see Luke 19:7). And, of course, Jesus was in the forefront.

What was happening? Jesus was passing through. When? Just before Palm Sunday. Why did Zacchaeus behave the way he did? He wanted to see Jesus. How did he do it? He ran ahead and climbed a tree.

We have already talked in chapter 7 of Jesus' own longing to set us free, to connect with us, to convince us we are His treasure and to give us lives of priestly purpose and holiness. Zacchaeus was targeted with these longings in mind. And so are you. Consider the following five ways Jesus approached the little man.

1. Jesus Was Purposeful

Luke 19:1 says that Jesus was "passing through." He was on His way to Jerusalem to die for all of our sins. A picture is drawn in this same gospel so we cannot miss the purposefulness of our Lord's intention. In Luke 9:51 it is reported: "As the time approached for him to be taken up to heaven, Jesus resolutely set out for Jerusalem." In some versions, it says "he set his face like flint." In other words, no one was going to change His mind. Later, Luke makes it even clearer. Just before the triumphal entry,

> Jesus took the Twelve aside and told them, "We are going up to Jerusalem, and everything that is written by the prophets about the Son of Man will be fulfilled. He will be handed over to the Gentiles. They will mock him, insult him, spit on him, flog him and kill him. On the third day he will rise again."
>
> Luke 18:31–33

Jesus was purposeful. He touched Zacchaeus' life on the way to the fulfillment of the prophecy. And He wants to touch your life, too.

2. Jesus Was Personal

Luke 19:5 says: "When Jesus reached the spot, he looked up and said to him, 'Zacchaeus.'" What did Jesus call him? He called the man by his name.

Do you believe that He knows your name? Have you ever heard Him call you by your name? Abraham did, and his response was "Here I am" (Genesis 22:1). Jacob heard God call and he answered, "Here I am" (Genesis 31:11). Moses recognized his name coming from the bush. He said, "Here I am" (Exodus 3:4). Samuel heard God call his name not once but three times and he answered, "Here I am" (1 Samuel 3:4, 6, 8). In the year that King Uzziah died, Isaiah heard God call his name and he said, "Here am I" (Isaiah 6:8). Saul—before he became the apostle Paul—heard God say, "Saul, Saul, why do you persecute me?" (Acts 9:4). Ananias heard his name called and he replied, "Yes, Lord" (Acts 9:10).

The precedent has been set. He knows our names. He calls to me. He calls to you. What is your answer? Will you persecute Him by putting cotton in your ears and doing your own thing, or will you say, "Here I am. Yes, Lord"?

3. Jesus Was Urgent

Jesus' word choices indicated urgency. Luke 19:5 records that He said *immediately* and *today*. I believe God is after us, He is serious about it and He wants the connection to happen now. Any mountain will do. Any tree will do, as long as we see Him. Now.

Have you been putting things off? "Tomorrow I will immerse myself in the Word." "I'll be glad to meet with You next Tuesday, Lord, to consider Your questions." The psalmist pleads, "Today, if you hear his voice, do not harden your hearts" (Psalm 95:7–8).

4. Jesus Had a Plan

"When Jesus reached the spot, he looked up" (Luke 19:5).

Tommy Tenney suggests that perhaps God put it in the heart of a farmer who lived decades before Zacchaeus walked the planet to plant a seedling in this spot. Someone else watered it and then He provided others to tend it. A sycamore-fig tree stood tall and strong—just right for climbing—at exactly the time Zacchaeus got the cue to scramble for his life-changing look at the Savior.

This is the spot God planned long ago. He did it for Zacchaeus and He did it for others. David testified: "All the days ordained for me were written in your book before one of them came to be" (Psalm 139:16). God told Jeremiah: "Before I formed you in the womb I knew you, before you were born I set you apart; I appointed you as a prophet to the nations" (Jeremiah 1:5). Later God assured Jeremiah that what He had said earlier was indeed true:

> "For I know the plans I have for you," declares the LORD, "plans to prosper you and not to harm you, plans to give you hope and a future. Then you will call upon me and come and pray to me, and I will listen to you. You will seek me and find me when you seek me with all your heart."
>
> Jeremiah 29:11–13

God did it for Zacchaeus, David, Jeremiah and you. He wants to offer you hope and a future. He wants you to seek Him with everything in you. He makes it possible to be found . . . by you at the spot of His choosing.

5. *Jesus Had a Servant's Heart*

Again, in Luke 19:5 we are told that Jesus "looked up" at Zacchaeus. Do you understand what a monumental thing that was? Because of Zacchaeus' physical stature, everyone looked down on him. And because of his chosen profession and his cheater's ways, the community abhorred him. But Jesus looked up. He purposefully placed Himself in a position that was beneath the man in the tree. At last, someone looked up at Zacchaeus.

That act of the Servant gave Zacchaeus the courage to come down from the tree and respond in a godly manner to the mutterers all around him who labeled him a sinner. Zacchaeus "stood up," and he spoke to the Lord, not to the mutterers. He offered generosity to those reviling him and proclaimed restitution on their behalf: "If I have cheated anybody out of anything, I will pay back four times the amount" (Luke 19:8).

Jesus came to the disciples as a Servant. He looked up at them while kneeling at the basin to wash their feet (see John 13:1–17). He looks up at you. He serves you. "Now that I, your Lord and Teacher, have washed your feet, you also should wash one another's feet. I have set you an example that you should do as I have done for you" (John 13:14–15).

Zacchaeus' Extreme Make-Over

Before his glimpse of Jesus, Zacchaeus was generous toward himself. He was a wealthy cheat. Afterward he was charitable toward others. The Law instructed Jews to make restitution of double for what was taken (see Exodus 22:4). But Zacchaeus paid back "four times the amount." Before the encounter, he had a position to protect. He was a chief tax collector, a plutocrat, attaining power and influence because of his wealth. After his glimpse, this cheating sinner had stature as a "son of Abraham" (Luke 19:9).

Son of Abraham was a title tossed around in those days to impress others. Jews defending their heritage would claim it. But John the Baptist put their self-righteous hearts to the task when he said this as they came forward for baptism: "Produce fruit in keeping with repentance. And do not begin to say to yourselves, 'We have Abraham as our father.' For I tell you that out of these stones God can raise up children for Abraham" (Luke 3:8).

Before the make-over, Zacchaeus was lost. Afterward, salvation came to his whole house because the "Son of Man came to seek and to save what was lost" (Luke 19:10). He was a short man physically, but after the encounter at the spot, Zacchaeus had a tall vision and he displayed fruit in keeping with repentance.

What would it take for you to get a glimpse of Jesus? Do you need to get closer? Or do you need to go higher? Do you need to get stuff out of the way? Do you need to be uninhibited? Do you need to ask God to draw you? Do you need to surrender to His call?

Zacchaeus was short. Where do you come up short in your goal of reaching Him? Desire? A plan of approach? Willingness? Confidence? Freedom?

If Jesus came to your house today, what would He find? How would He view the workroom of your gifts and talents? Do the relationships in your family room honor Him? How about the library of your thoughts? What about the dining room of your appetites? What about all the secrets hiding in the attic?

Moses climbed a mountain and saw God. Abraham looked up on Mount Moriah and saw God. Zacchaeus climbed a tree and saw God. Will you come up higher and see more of God?

Searching for More

1. Name one "chosen spot" or defining moment in your spiritual journey.
2. In the Christian disciplines, do you gravitate more toward the line of duty or the delight of God? How do you know?
3. What choices are you making that reduce your desire for God?
4. Choose any of the five ways that Jesus approached Zacchaeus and share how He has exhibited that action in your life. (He was purposeful. He was personal. He was urgent. He had a plan. He had a servant's heart.)

5. How is God in the process of an extreme make-over in your life?

6. If Jesus came to your house today, what would He find? Choose one of the rooms to discuss (workroom, family room, library, dining room, attic). (For reference see Bob Munger's "My Heart—Christ's Home" or Lyman Coleman, ed., *Serendipity New Testament for Groups* [Nashville: Serendipity House, 1990], Luke 19:1–10.)

P A R T 4

deeper

The River of God

"Where the river flows everything will live."

Ezekiel 47:9

10

Take the Plunge

ake the plunge. The water is wild, but you'll love it."
That was all I needed to dive in headfirst. The ocean
waves were high, but I was a confident swimmer. It did not
take long, however, to realize that this was more than a five-
foot-two-inch grandmother had bargained for. I should have
noticed that only the men were in the rough water.

As I was about to swim back to shore, a wave crashed
over my head. My face popped up in the water, but before
I could catch my breath, another monster loomed. It, too,
broke over me and this time I rose, flailing, to the surface.
Then a third breaker tossed my body, easily now, like a
careless salad chef. I thought: *This is it. And they're not even
going to know what happened to me.*

Meanwhile, our daughter, Joy, her husband, Tom, and
their two-year-old son, Kyle, were standing on the shore
watching me turn flips in the briny deep. They were all

151

having a good laugh at my expense until our son-in-law realized that I was really in trouble.

Out he ran—all six-foot-four, 250 pounds of him. He grabbed whatever limb he could seize and pulled me to safety. I was coughing and spitting up saltwater and then realized, to my horror, that things that should have been in my bathing suit were not. The best part, though, was that my grandson watched with a wide grin, amazed with the wonder of it all. With twinkling eyes, he said: "Meemaw, do it again!"

As you might imagine, this story has provided much entertainment with me as the brunt of family humor, and I deserve much of it. But I thought, *If I'm going to have to endure continued humiliation in the retelling, perhaps God could use it. Do you suppose there's a message in there—anywhere?*

We serve a faithful God and He did not let me down. Another dimension of God's love is its depth; in other words, His love is as deep as the ocean. And if I take the plunge and jump into the depths with Him, I can count on three certainties. And, I dare say, so can you:

1. The ride is wilder than anything you will ever experience.
2. You will be exposed in unimaginable ways.
3. Immature people will ask you to continue doing religious tricks. But no amount of ecclesiastical gymnastics can substitute for going to the depths of God.

I wanted to understand, so I asked God to show me more. What promises does He offer those who jump into His ocean or His river of love? What impediments might we face? My discovery changed my life. Perhaps what I learned will help you, too, grow spiritually in this fourth dimension. For those who persevere, His rewards are enticing.

First let me point out that the river of God is mentioned all through the Bible. From Genesis to Revelation, it is prominent. Consider a few examples. Genesis 2:10 states: "A river watering the garden flowed from Eden; from there it was separated into four headwaters." In Revelation 22:1–2, John gives this account.

> Then the angel showed me the river of the water of life, as clear as crystal, flowing from the throne of God and of the Lamb down the middle of the great street of the city. On each side of the river stood the tree of life, bearing twelve crops of fruit, yielding its fruit every month. And the leaves of the tree are for the healing of the nations.

The psalmists and prophets wrote of this river. The Sons of Korah penned these words: "There is a river whose streams make glad the city of God, the holy place where the Most High dwells" (Psalm 46:4). God's invitation in Isaiah says: "Come, all you who are thirsty, come to the waters" (55:1). Probably the fullest account of the river of God was recorded by Ezekiel:

> The man brought me back to the entrance of the temple, and I saw water coming out from under the threshold of the temple toward the east (for the temple faced east). The water was coming down from under the south side of the temple, south of the altar. He then brought me out through the north gate and led me around the outside to the outer gate facing east, and the water was flowing from the south side.
>
> As the man went eastward with a measuring line in his hand, he measured off a thousand cubits and then led me through water that was ankle-deep. He measured off an-

other thousand cubits and led me through water that was knee-deep. He measured off another thousand and led me through water that was up to the waist. He measured off another thousand, but now it was a river that I could not cross, because the water had risen and was deep enough to swim in—a river that no one could cross.

Ezekiel 47:1–5

If you have read this book to this point, you are serious about growing spiritually. You have already heeded God's invitation to come to His feast and you have probably gotten rid of some of your entanglements and expectations so that you can run His race with perseverance. You have realized God's heart is to woo you higher because there is more of Him than you thought. And now you long to take the plunge—growing in yet another dimension of His love.

Your spiritual age is not a factor in this swim. If you are young in the Lord, your enthusiasm counts for much. If you have known Jesus for many years, there is always a deeper place to go. Paul says, "Oh, the depth of the riches both of the wisdom and knowledge of God! How unsearchable are His judgments and unfathomable His ways!" (Romans 11:33, NASB). If they are unfathomable, then you can shirk what Calvin Miller calls "birdbath living" and go even deeper.

In his book *Into the Depths of God* (Bethany, 2000), Miller tells of his family's adventure at the Great Barrier Reef:

My son had come to scuba dive while my wife and I snorkeled.

Snorkeling is a pastime more than a sport. For while my son plunged deeply beneath clear waters to bury himself in the wonder of the mysterious ocean depths, my wife and I, wearing masks, only floated on the surface facedown.

In some ways what we were all seeing looked the same. But my wife and I literally sunburned our backs in our surface study of the reef, while our son plumbed its wonders.

What amazes me most is what we reported upon returning from the Great Barrier Reef. Ask me if I've been there, and I will hastily answer yes. So will my son. However, the truth is that the content of our experience was greatly different. We will both spend the rest of our lives talking about that experience and our enthusiasm will always be exuberant. But only our son really knew the Reef; only he understood the issue of depth.

Do you want to go deeper? Let's begin with impediments and then view our rewards.

Problems with Going to the Depths

There are at least seven issues that might lure us away from the river of God. See if you identify with any of these.

1. The Control Issue

For many years our family enjoyed an annual four-generation trek to the Outer Banks of North Carolina. It never failed. The six-hour drive begged wriggling toes to escape from socks to play footsie with the foam. I could not wait. "Are we there yet?" As soon as possible, I would spring out of the car, run to the shore and wade in ankle-deep.

This brings up a few questions. If you are in the water ankle-deep, are you in the water? The answer is a decided yes. At this point, are you in control of the water or is the water in control of you? Generally that is not enough depth for you to lose your poise. The deeper you go in the water, however, the less control you have.

155

Ankle-deep? Still in control. Knee-deep? A little less power over the water. Waist-high? You are at the mercy of waves. And swimming? Now the current will move you where it will. The same is true in going to the depths of God. The deeper you go the less control you have, and many who call Jesus "Lord" cannot handle that.

That was true of me in regard to the Holy Spirit. I called Jesus Savior and Lord, but I told Him what I would receive from Him and what I would not. He gently, but firmly, nudged me to realize that if I was giving direction then I was not surrendering control. I knew I could trust Him to give or withhold anything that would bring Him the greatest glory. So I took my hands off of my demands.

It is my observation that there are not many human beings who do not struggle with some control issues. Most of us will organize and manipulate in order to retain power that is not really ours. If you want to go to the depths of God, you will have to surrender control.

2. The "Look Good" Issue

I have a friend named June who owns a home on the Severn River in Annapolis, Maryland. The pool in her back-yard overlooks the scenic waters that wind their way around the U.S. Naval Academy en route to the Chesapeake Bay.

One summer day a number of friends were invited to a pool party. All the women, donning new bathing suits and perfectly coifed hair, sat at pool's edge. I looked pretty good, too. But it was driving me crazy to sit poolside with just my feet dangling in the water. Once in a while I reached down with my hand to swoop and swirl little ripples, but I wanted all of me to dive in. This created a dilemma.

I could stay in my "looking good" mode, and miss the pleasure of the water. Or I could dive in and enjoy the encounter with the water to its fullest, but afterward I would look like a drowned rat while everyone else looked perfect. Finally I could stand it no longer—I jumped in. I stopped caring that I would look dreadful upon resurfacing.

Do you see that sometimes the reason we will not go to the depths with God is because we are afraid of looking bad to those watching? Let me give you another example from a morning in church.

It was a magnificent time of worship. We were singing of God's holiness and I felt that He was asking me to get on my knees. I peeked around sheepishly and realized no one else was on his or her knees. I felt it my duty to report that to God. Still He persisted. *Marilyn, get on your knees. You're standing on holy ground.*

"But, Lord . . ."

To my shame I made a bargain with God that morning. "If they sing the song again and mention the word *holy*, I'll know it's You and that You really want me on my knees." The worship team sang the song for another five minutes and said the word *holy* many times. I got on my knees and, to my knowledge, no one cared if I knelt or not. But God noticed.

3. The Fear Issue

Sometimes fear can keep you from taking the plunge in any endeavor. Let's look again at swimming in the ocean. When a huge wave is coming straight at you, which is best: Turn and swim toward shore as fast as you can, or face the wave and dive right into the middle of it?

The answer, of course, is to square off with it. Dive right in. In *My Utmost for His Highest*, Oswald Chambers says: "The surf that distresses the ordinary swimmer produces in the surf-rider the super-joy of going clean through it."

Fear forces us to run the other way from whatever it is that makes us scared. What might make you fearful of going to the depths with God? Is it what He might ask of you? Are you afraid that you do not have what it takes? That others might ridicule you? If you identify with this problem of fear, then ask God to help you understand what is scaring you off. Meet your fear. Dive down. As your encounter with Him grows, your fears will vanish.

4. The Humility Issue

One of my favorite sports to watch is Olympic diving. My father was a professional diver and although, nowadays, the maneuvers are far more sophisticated, I still recognize some of the moves he would showcase to me as a wide-eyed child.

A perfect score of ten in the Olympics is achieved by only a few, and one of the determining factors for such excellence is how the diver enters the water. A splash draws negative attention; the less amount of splash, the better.

If we are honest, most of us walk through the Christian life hoping we will draw a little attention—at least a few approving nods; in other words, we don't mind a little splash now and then. But the more we dive into the depths of the Almighty, the more we find ourselves content to be unobserved and the less we worry about being noticed. An incident in my life shows what I mean.

I love to do calligraphy. I find great joy in carefully planning and penning each letter of a chosen Bible verse and giving the finished product, a framed illumination, to a friend. One weekend our church had a garage sale to benefit the missions program. One table hosted giveaways. On that table was one of my pieces given as a gift years before.

I did not realize that until the next morning in church when our new pastor, who had claimed it, held it up for all to see. He was excited because the verse highlighted the sermon text he had chosen for the worship service. He saw it as a confirmation, but it made my heart fall. The best I had to offer was on the throwaway table. But God reminded me seconds later that although someone else had discarded it, He was using it.

God is looking for those who do not need to make a big splash.

Could it be that pride is a deterrent for you to overcome?

5. The Relationship Issue

When I was a child there were two nonnegotiable swimming rules: (1) You could not dive in until waiting at least thirty minutes after eating; and (2) you could not—under any circumstances—swim alone.

The second rule teaches us something important about going to the depths with God: Sometimes our relationships will help us get there. Or, put another way, sometimes we do not go to the depths with God because no one encourages us in our desire to do so.

Do you have a mentor? What about an accountability partner? Do most of your friends support you? Or do they think your continuous passion to know Christ is a bit suspicious? Do they frown on what you are becoming? Do they consistently point out dangers of the reef to dissuade you? Do they show you only one-dimensional maps and charts of the unfathomable—lots of data—or do they tell you exciting tales of the nooks and crannies they have seen in the depths themselves?

Solomon's wisdom shines here: "Two are better than one, because they have a good return for their work: If one falls down, his friend can help him up. But pity the man who falls and has no one to help him up!" (Ecclesiastes 4:9–10).

The prophet Amos adds: "Can two walk together, except they be agreed?" (Amos 3:3, KJV).

We were never meant to swim alone. Relationships matter.

6. The Willingness Issue

My young friend Kristin shared with me that there was a time when the thought of swimming in the ocean terrified her. That surprised me because now she loves it.

I asked, "How did you become willing to try it?"

She smiled. "Oh, that was easy. First, my dad carried me in and then, when I felt comfortable with that, he held my hand. Then he stood beside me, and now I'm free to jump in all by myself."

God wants us to be willing to meet Him in the depths. He will carry us, hold our hands, stand alongside and give us the freedom to see Him there. Why? Because He wants to connect with us in the depths of His love even more than we do.

Our prayers can echo King David's: "Restore to me the joy of your salvation and grant me a willing spirit, to sustain me" (Psalm 51:12).

7. The Temperature Issue

Sometimes, even on a nice day, the ocean temperature can be on the cold side. It is not hard, if you had plans of swimming on one of those days, to dip your toe into the water and have a change of heart. And many who decide to go ahead and enjoy the ocean usually torture themselves by going into the cold water gingerly. They put a toe in and jump back with a good shiver. Then they get a little braver and go in further only to retreat with teeth chattering. In essence, they turn the whole process into agony.

The best way to handle the temperature issue is to run full steam ahead from the shore and . . . just jump in. The ones already in the water are usually the first to yell, "Come on in. The water's fine."

It is the same spiritually: Sometimes the atmosphere around us is icy. People are cool to our passion for God or indifferent to the Gospel. One dip of our toes and we decide not to press it, not to offend, not to move deeper with God after all. But do you know what? If there is coldness around, it matters not. It is best in that situation just to take the plunge and call others to join you there. It is the lukewarm bathers who grieve God's heart, the ones who cannot seem to make up their minds about going in because of conditions around them.

Just jump in.

View from the River

One summer recently, John and I went to Lone Peak near Bozeman, Montana, for a week's vacation with old friends. We decided to float down the Madison River on inner tubes, leisurely, taking a whole afternoon to do it. New insights about the river of God became plentiful.

We noticed, first of all, how the cars on the road parallel to the river whizzed by, oblivious to the fact that there was a river, let alone people in it. Whether from ignorance or familiarity, they gave the impression in their haste that the charms of the river held no significance for them. It seemed as though they were in a rut, moving fast and wearing blinders.

I could not help thinking of how this resembles our culture. Look at Paul's words in 2 Corinthians 4:4: "The god of this age has blinded the minds of unbelievers, so that they cannot see the light of the gospel of the glory of Christ, who is the image of God." There are many lost souls, ignorant of God's passion to love them. Others are all too familiar with churches that offer programs but not the presence of God. In either case, they are not in the water; nor are they too impressed with those who are.

On a long float, there are many things to observe. We also noticed that not everyone was oblivious to the presence of the river and our happy band floating along in it. We watched people—and wild horses—watching us. Some of those people were enjoying picnics on shore, some were playing ball and some were just gawking at us.

The point is, they were spectators, not participants. They were not in the water. I paused to think what might entice them to get in. Maybe if we splashed and laughed, they would see how much fun it all was and jump in. Or perhaps we could link our tubes together in a show of solidarity, showing them that the river offered a place to belong with friends.

But, really, the only thing worthy of drawing them in was the wonder of the river itself. Nothing we did would make much of a difference.

I believe that if you are reading this book, you are already in the river. You have said yes to God's initiative—maybe a long time ago. Now I challenge you to consider encouraging the interest of spectators. The way to do this is not to show them how much fun you are having or that the river is just a place to gather.

Jesus said, "But I, when I am lifted up from the earth, will draw all men to myself" (John 12:32). Rather than ask,

"How might I draw spectators to become participants?" the appropriate question is, "How can I lift up the wonders of the God of the river?" Our part is to lift Him up. His part is to draw people.

Our pleasant journey was not without physical challenges. Once in a while, a rock would surprise us, seeming to leap up from nowhere. A further surprise was the fact that in this otherwise crystal clean river, stagnant places around the rocks and boulders were slimy and smelly. If your tube got stuck there, you had to push and pull your way out of the muck.

I soon learned that I could either smash into the boulders or use them to push off of. If I stayed there, my situation had the smell of death and became more disagreeable with passing minutes.

Those rocks are like the hard places in our lives. For our family, for instance, that would be the many challenges we have faced with two of our three children being diabetic. Sometimes I smashed into problems created by the disease and could not seem to get out of the stagnant waters. But our faithful God met us and showed us how to use the difficulties to push us back into the current of the Holy Spirit; we learned that we always felt better after the challenge than we had before it.

Thus, juvenile diabetes was first an enemy, then a teacher and finally a gift. Why? Because it is what God used to show us to depend on Him, to pray as a couple of scared parents, to be more disciplined than we would have been without it and far more sensitive to the needs of others. Rocks are hard and often immovable. Perfect for pushing off of.

And finally, we realized that after four hours of exposure to wind and sun, we were dehydrated. Our mouths were parched and our skin pocked with deep, dry cracks. When we go the depths, it is wise to take gulps of living water regularly. Jesus said, "Whoever drinks the water I give him will never thirst. Indeed, the water I give him will become in him a spring of water welling up to eternal life" (John 4:14).

Rewards of the Plunge

Because God so longs for us to know His depths, He makes it most attractive. I could not pretend to know what you need in your life as you read this, but I do know that going deeper with Him offers much to touch your need. I do not think it would be wise to go deeper just to get the rewards, but great things happen as we meet with Him at a deeper level.

Consider these verses from Ezekiel 47:6–12 to see what wonders await us in the depths:

He asked me, "Son of man, do you see this?"

Then he led me back to the bank of the river. When I arrived there, I saw a great number of trees on each side of the river. He said to me, "This water flows toward the eastern region and goes down into the Arabah, where it enters the Sea. When it empties into the Sea, the water there becomes fresh. Swarms of living creatures will live wherever the river flows. There will be large numbers of fish, because this water flows there and makes the salt water fresh; so where the river flows everything will live. Fishermen will stand along the shore; from En Gedi to En Eglaim there will be places for spreading nets. The fish will be of many kinds—like the fish of the Great Sea. But the swamps and marshes will not become fresh; they will be left for salt. Fruit trees of all kinds will grow on both banks of the river. Their leaves will not wither, nor will their fruit fail. Every month they will bear, because the water from the sanctuary flows to them. Their fruit will serve for food and their leaves for healing."

Ezekiel 47:6–12

God is asking you, "Child, do you see this?" In verse eight the Creator of all declares that where this water flows the saltwater will become fresh. It would be no big deal for fresh water to become salty. But to reverse the result and make briny water become fresh requires a complicated chemical interaction. God is saying that going to the depths with Him makes transformation possible. Is that needed in your life?

He also states that "where the river flows everything will live" (verse 9). Have you been yearning for life and vitality? A bounce in your step and a song in your heart? Jesus told us: "I have come that they may have life, and have it to the full" (John 10:10). So we should not be surprised when plunging into the depths with Him brings life. Ruts eliminated. Dullness shunned. Blandness cast off.

Ezekiel also says there will be "swarms of living creatures" and "large numbers of fish." Plenty is another part of the package. And I think He is speaking of plenty of Him. Think about it. Jesus is the light of the world. That is enough illumination for your life and mine. Jesus is the gate. That is enough access. He is the good shepherd. That is enough refuge and protection. Jesus is the resurrection and the life. That is enough power. He is the way—enough direction; the truth—enough stability; the life—enough vitality. He is the true vine. That is plenty of motivation for fruitfulness and growth. And He is the bread of life—enough sustenance.

Consider phrases from verse 12. They support the idea that going with our God to the depths offers us such plenty. They say that the fruit of their trees will not fail and "every

165

month they will bear." That is another way of saying He offers fruitfulness. When God says that the "fruit will serve for food," He is underscoring the fact that this growth gives us sustenance. And His supply abounds. There will be "fruit trees of all kinds" and "leaves [that] will not wither." Is healing needed in your life right now physically, emotionally, mentally, relationally, financially, spiritually? He offers that, too! "Their leaves [will serve] for healing."

It is equally amazing that one of the results of being with Him in the depths is our growing desire to tell others about it. "Fishermen will stand along the shore" because there are "places for spreading nets." We truly can be fishers of men, shouting the invitation with glee: "Come on in! The water's great."

God will never make us take the plunge. Ezekiel 47:11 says "the swamps and marshes will not become fresh; they will be left for salt." The "will not" of that verse makes me think that, if swamps and marshes had feet, they would stomp them in defiance. Even with the promise of transformation, life, freshness, plenty, growth, fruitfulness, sustenance and healing, some will still say, "No, thank you." It makes me think of Jesus' warning in Matthew 5:13: "You are the salt of the earth. But if the salt loses its saltiness, how can it be made salty again? It is no longer good for anything, except to be thrown out and trampled by men."

God has issued His invitation yet again, and I am wondering where you are. I know you are not oblivious to the river or you would not be reading this book. And I believe you are a participant, not a spectator. But are you in ankle-deep, knee-high, waist-high or in over your head? Would you consider asking the Holy Spirit to help you make a true assessment? And would you ask God to help you move to the next place?

Are you flowing freely in the Spirit's current or dawdling at water's edge? Are you crashing into rocks or pushing off of them? And if you are still not moving toward the depths, which of the issues has you caught in stagnant water: Control? Looking good? Pride? Fear? Relationships? Unwillingness? Inability to overcome the cold?

It is watershed time. It is no longer appropriate to be reading about going to the depths without going to the depths. If you have been in over your head for a while and you are tired, then turn over, float and look up. And if you are ready to take the plunge, I will say to you what I overheard two twelve-year-old boys say to each other at the pool last summer:

"Hey, you! I'll race you to the deep end!"

Searching for More

1. How have you experienced any of the three certainties of going deeper with God?

      _____ The ride is wild.
      _____ You are exposed in amazing ways.
      _____ Immature people ask you to continue doing "religious tricks."

2. Which of the problems with going to the depths do you experience most? Explain your answer.

      _____ The control issue
      _____ The "look good" issue
      _____ The fear issue
      _____ The humility issue
      _____ The relationship issue

_____ The willingness issue
_____ The temperature issue

3. Where are you in the river of God and where do you want to be? Explain your answer.

_____ Ankle-deep
_____ Knee-deep
_____ Up to the waist
_____ Swimming
_____ In a stagnant pool
_____ Crashing into rocks
_____ Pushing off rocks
_____ Inviting others in
_____ Racing to the deep end
_____ Other

4. What rewards of the plunge appeal to you most? Why?

_____ Freshness
_____ Transformation
_____ Full life
_____ Plenty of Him
_____ Growth
_____ Fruitfulness
_____ Sustenance and food
_____ Healing
_____ Variety
_____ A desire to be a "fisher of men"

11

Deeper Intimacy

The Ironman Triathlon World Championship is aptly named for those athletes who dare to enter Hawaii's grueling competition. First, contestants swim nearly two and a half miles in the ocean, then they bike more than a hundred miles atop volcanic turf, then they run a bit farther than a normal 26-mile marathon. This event is not for the faint of heart—nor the casual athlete. The rigors of training, energy and sacrifice that these men and women endure are grueling. Usually this is an event for individual competitors, but recently a team entry made history.

Dick and Rick Hoyt, father and son, entered the ranks of triathletes in 1999. This duo took on the competition as a personal challenge. Rick, born in the 1960s, has cerebral palsy and has never been able to move well or even speak. Modern technology has offered him a way of communicating through computers. Although his challenges are diverse, he is a college graduate and has a keen sense of adventure.

His father, Dick, is a great motivator, physically fit and sufficient for most challenges. Rick began asking Dick to wheel him across the finish line in several local charity events.

It was not long before the heart of this adventurous son dared his dad to enter the Ironman. Taking the plunge in the ocean for the first leg, father pulled son behind him in a raft through the breakers that overwhelm the strongest of swimmers. Another gizmo was rigged for the torturous biking leg. And then the marathon. Their aim, of course, was not to win or even to compete with other entrants. They wanted to complete the course—and complete they did. Because this father took on himself the strenuous physical and mental challenges of their mission, Team Hoyt crossed the finish line. Only one thing eclipsed Rick's grin. It was the smile on his father's face.

Up to this point in the book you may have wondered if coming to the feast, running the race, scaling the mountain and plunging the depths of God is all about your effort. It is not! We cannot approach Him or run alongside Him or gaze upon Him or know any of His unfathomable ways without His divine aid—direction, guidance and strength. Only He is sufficient and powerful enough to expend the effort and sacrifice needed to conclude the journey. In Jesus it is finished. Isaiah said it well: "Lord, you establish peace for us; all that we have accomplished you have done for us" (Isaiah 26:12). As we feast and run and climb and dive, intimacy happens and God smiles.

The Depth of Gratitude

Intimacy. Reaching the deepest places of God's heart. It is a dimension in which nothing is held back for those who long to plunge into the unfathomable depths of His love. Worship happens, the reason for it all.

Few places in the Bible picture this desperation for intimacy with God and its resultant worship of God more than the story of the sinful woman who anointed Jesus' feet. She had a goal to accomplish, and in reaching it she shows us how to persevere, to face great barriers, to let nothing stand in the way of our desire to go to the depths of intimacy with God. Let's follow her story, beginning with these words from Scripture:

> Now one of the Pharisees invited Jesus to have dinner with him, so he went to the Pharisee's house and reclined at the table. When a woman who had lived a sinful life in that town learned that Jesus was eating at the Pharisee's house, she brought an alabaster jar of perfume, and as she stood behind him at his feet weeping, she began to wet his feet with her tears. Then she wiped them with her hair, kissed them and poured perfume on them.
>
> Luke 7:36–38

Here was a woman who plunged in with total abandon. She surrendered her all to the One who gave His all. In doing so, she called God's feast *worship.* The new race marked out for her was labeled *worship.* She saw His glory in the heights of His love and fell facedown—in *worship.* And now in her devotion, humbly at His feet, she experienced time in the depths of Him as pure *worship.* In Jesus all was complete. Finished. Everything else was loss compared to the surpassing greatness of knowing Him. The look on His face was worth everything to her.

As Matt Redman says in *The Unquenchable Worshipper* (Regal, 2001), "It was the worship of a woman who didn't know the rules—an unpredictable, untamed heart on a quest to see Jesus glorified." She was unbridled. She had nothing to lose and everything to gain. She was the consummate picture of both a tough girl and a party girl ... but repentant. And she embarrassed everyone; everyone but Jesus. She crashed a dinner party. She mingled with guests of the opposite sex. She let her hair down and she did the work of a common household slave. Unthinkable. But she was loved and accepted by Jesus so nothing else mattered.

Who was this woman and why was her life winsome? She was not a princess or the daughter of a respected priest or a prophetess. Some scholars think this woman was a prostitute. What we know for sure is that she "lived a sinful life" (Luke 7:37). But before you dismiss her with the no-accounts and the riffraff, stay with me to see how this one traded her illegitimate loves for one pure and holy passion. How this one who looked for love in all the wrong places experienced a touch from the true source of love.

It is astounding to notice what she did not come to Jesus with. She did not come with words or programs or requests for blessing, or rituals or complaints, announcements or lists. She came with a grateful heart, wanting to bring an offering to the One who had loved her so freely. Open hands. No agenda. Just adoration that led to deepest intimacy. And you can be like her.

The Response to Lavish Love

The adoration that this woman offered Jesus demonstrates that in the quiet place of His heart we lose ourselves and worship Him. Still, her actions surprised the host and most of the guests. How was her devotion received? Let's view the other participants in this scene.

The Response of Jesus

Jesus received the ministry of this woman who wept at His feet with no questions asked. He knew the woman's heart was repentant and searching and, in return, He offered her, as my songwriter friend Kelly Willie says, "a gown, a crown and a mansion uptown." Jesus was gifting the woman lavishly with robes of righteousness, a crown of life and a place in His mansions prepared for her in eternity. No wonder she longed to give Him her all.

Jesus' love helped the woman realize that we cannot be desperate about the Savior until we are desperate about our own sin. And we will never be desperate about our own sin until we stop being desperate about everybody else's sin.

Many Bible greats underscore this truth. Jeremiah wrote that the "heart is deceitful above all things. . . . Who can understand it?" (Jeremiah 17:9). Paul said he was the worst of sinners (see 1 Timothy 1:15). Isaiah lamented: "Woe to me! . . . I am a man of unclean lips, and I live among a people of unclean lips" (Isaiah 6:5). Job confessed: "I despise myself and repent in dust and ashes" (Job 42:6). David begged: "Create in me a pure heart" (Psalm 51:10). This was not just sorrow about missing the mark; it was comprehension that ours is a sin nature.

Jesus could invite that kind of honest look at oneself because His love overpowered all that the sin nature stirred up. He delighted in the woman's coming near, in her whole-hearted desire to express her devotion.

The Pharisees and Temple authorities had convinced many that the Messiah would be a rule-giver, a rule-keeper and a rule-enforcer. He would be a person of decorum and majesty, an ideal of their making. As a result, they taught that he would not associate with tax collectors or sinners, and certainly not stained women.

173

But Jesus broke all the rules. He did not wag fingers in anybody's face and He dined with the worst of sinners. In fact, He sought them out. It was clear: This Messiah colored outside the lines. He is who He is and not as any Pharisee, then or now, would want Him to be. Jesus rewrote the script on the Messiah.

Jesus' love made a place for the woman. Jesus' love made a place for me. And Jesus' love makes a place for you, too. Why? Because He longs for deeper intimacy with us.

The Response of the Dinner Host

Just when all is going according to plan in any drama, another protagonist or two appears. They are usually Snidely Whiplash types with selfish dispositions and unworthy causes to promote. In this case the damsel had met the true lover of her soul—Jesus—and up jump the Pharisees with sneers and jeers, twirling their black moustaches with relish. Remember the "long faces, long robes, long ledgers and long lists"?

The host, Simon, was a Pharisee and I have wondered why he invited Jesus in the first place. Curiosity? An object to ridicule? A dare? Or maybe an unarticulated need. Other gospel accounts tell of a Pharisee named Simon offering hospitality to Jesus, and that Simon was a leper (see Matthew 26:6–13; Mark 14:3–9). We do not know if this was the same individual or not, but perhaps this host was also longing for One who would have the courage to reach out to him with healing and transformation. One who would love him unconditionally.

In that case, Simon had a problem. Being well versed in the Law, he knew that prophets were not supposed to come in contact with unholy things—especially women of the night (see 1 Corinthians 6:15). This thought about

Jesus ran through his mind: "If this man were a prophet, he would know who is touching him and what kind of woman she is—that she is a sinner" (Luke 7:39).

Why was Jesus letting this woman touch Him? Did He not know the Law? That could not be possible because Jesus clearly taught as one having authority; He had shown astonishing insight about the Law from the time He was a child. Did Jesus not get it? Did He not understand that this woman was nothing but trouble?

Was it possible, then, that Jesus actually saw the woman clean? And, if that was possible, perhaps Jesus could see Simon clean, too.

What a conundrum! Simon might have wanted to draw close to Jesus, but his role as a Pharisee required him to watch the rules, pronounce dictates and point fingers—even at himself. He had his reputation to protect, so the abandonment that God produced so evidently in the woman was foreign to him. Simon concluded that Jesus was not a prophet; Simon was the one who did not get it.

Jesus is God and He knew Simon's thoughts. The Master then told Simon a parable about two men who were forgiven different-sized debts and the resultant difference in their love for the forgiving moneylender. It was perfect for the delivery of zinging candor: "He who has been forgiven little loves little" (Luke 7:47).

All Simon could see was the woman's sin. And because he was so busy pointing out her mistakes and defending his image, he could not see his own need. This Pharisee praised himself for his insight; Jesus condemned him for misjudging his sinfulness. The woman condemned herself for her sinful life; Jesus praised her for acknowledging her need. Then He told her that her many sins were forgiven.

This account indicates that we will not know grace unless, and until, we know we need grace. The Pharisee was as big a sinner as the woman, maybe even more so in our eyes, but he did not know it. The more we surrender to the God of grace and mercy, the more we see Him and ourselves with clarity, the more we receive His love and the more we love Him back.

One word of caution: We can have a religious spirit about people with religious spirits. We need to look at ourselves. I believe there is a Pharisee in each of us. Ask God to reveal where you have a long face, a long ledger and a long list and I suspect you will find, as I have, a Pharisee looking back at you in the mirror.

The Other Guests

Guest lists are fairly predictable. Usually there are a number of close friends for comfort. Then a few people the host owes. A number of work associates are included and often a scene-stealer or two—you know, a clown or someone of importance in the eyes of the other guests.

We are not told who else attended this party, other than the "other guests." Judging from other accounts of dinner parties hosted by Pharisees, there were likely other Pharisees in attendance and some disciples, too. But at this point, none of them got it either. They wondered among themselves about the Man who forgives sins: "Who is this?" they asked (Luke 7:49).

While the Pharisees had their fingers wagging, the other guests had their tongues wagging.

Love's Language: Worship

Regardless of who attended, it is clear that the spotlight was on this woman. This one who fell at Jesus' feet teaches us how to worship facedown. Indulge my use of an acrostic to expand our understanding of her search for intimacy with God. The word *worship* will serve to reveal some important insights.

W

The woman *waited* and *watched* and *went* where Jesus was. Luke 7:37 says: "When a woman who had lived a sinful life in that town learned that Jesus was eating at the Pharisee's house, she brought an alabaster jar of perfume." I had to repent when I read this. How often have I have been somewhere, even in times of ministry, and expected God to wait and watch and come to me . . . on command, no less? Now I am learning to ask, "Show me where You are already working, Lord, and give me grace to come alongside Your longing." Would you consider asking the same thing?

O

The woman brought an *offering*. The text does not say that she asked for anything; she brought something and she gave generously. She did not submit a wish list or rattle off a litany of complaints. This picture compelled me to ask another hard question: When have I come to God for what I could get—how He could make my life work better—rather than what I could offer Him to please His heart? What about you?

R

The woman was *real*. No pretense. No cover-up. She lived a sinful life "in that town" and she went to Jesus "in that town." I have an esteemed friend with a lesbian past. She is now happily married to the man of her dreams. When she talks of her long road to wholeness and intimacy with her Savior, she describes herself as "the whore who sits at Jesus' feet." That is being real.

I know my heart to be dark, too, and I am desperate to confess my sin so that I can be in His holy presence and know His love. And I am repenting about my attention to other peoples' sins that obscures acknowledgement of my personal transgressions. I invite you to do the same. Would you join me in realizing that there is not one of us who has our act all together? We are, in fact, all "whores" lusting after lesser lovers (see Ezekiel 16). But I can choose to sit at Jesus' feet and so can you. Sometimes we worship Him best when we are real.

S

The woman gave a *sumptuous* gift. She was lavish, extravagant and uninhibited. She did not just wash Jesus' feet; she shed tears on them, wiped them with her hair, kissed them and poured perfume on them—all things that cost her personally. Her anointing did not escape the onlookers' raised eyebrows. In other biblical accounts where Jesus is anointed with perfume, the onlookers generally consider it a colossal waste. In one scene Judas grumbles that the perfume could have been sold and the money given to the poor (see John 12:5). Jesus tells him to be quiet and leave the giver alone. He gives of Himself lavishly, and I believe He longs for us to do the same.

My worship is too often *inhibited*. The only difference between the words *inhibited* and *inhabited* is a big *I* right in the middle of them. If I appointed an *A* for *Almighty* to replace it, perhaps I would be inhabited by His presence. Are you stingy with your devotion to Him or are you "poured out like a drink offering," as Paul suggests in Philippians 2:17?

H

The woman was *humble*. Luke 7:38 says "she stood behind him at his feet weeping." She stooped in back of Jesus. She approached His feet. She cried. This is body language that declares humility. It makes me think of the parable of the wheat and weeds (see Matthew 13:24–30). Do you know why the owner of the field directed the caretaker to wait until harvest time to separate the two? Others have suggested it was because then the plants would be mature. The weeds would take a proud stance. Tall. Unbending. The wheat, with full heads on the stalks, would bow. *Maturity* is spelled *h-u-m-i-l-i-t-y*.

How often has my pride haughtily careened for position before God seated on His throne? And I wonder: Have I tried to bump Him off the seat of majesty and honor altogether? Have you?

I

The woman was *immediate* in her response. She did not ponder convenience or comfort. She knew where Jesus was and she went to Him. Right then. She did not care about the opinions of others and she did not miss the moment. *Carpe diem.* Seize the day. I am sure I have fumbled meeting with Him in His presence because of hesitation. Do you tarry when He calls?

P

She was *persistent*. As Jesus enumerated His comparisons of the woman with His pharisaical dinner host, He said, "You did not give me a kiss, but this woman, from the time I entered, has not stopped kissing my feet" (Luke 7:45). Has not stopped, indeed. Oh, that I would have such a heart of steadfast devotion for the faithful one! Oh, that you and I might become unrelenting facedown worshipers as well!

My challenge to you is this: Risk worshiping the Lamb of God in the manner of this woman. Watch and wait for Him. Offer what would please His heart. If you do not know what that is, ask Him. Be real. Be sumptuous, lavish in your love. Practice humility. Be immediate. And persist.

Why?

"Worthy is the Lamb, who was slain, to receive power and wealth and wisdom and strength and honor and glory and praise!" (Revelation 5:12).

Because this sinful woman was forgiven much, she loved much. Because God first loved her and convinced her of that, she was able to look at her own life with honesty and find affirmation, even in the darkest places. She feasted. She ran the race. She climbed the mountain. And in her freedom she plunged the depths. In a word, she understood intimacy with God.

Where Are You?

Our journey together is nearing completion. Are you growing more secure in intimacy with each passing day? Are you kneeling with this woman at Jesus' feet—convinced of God's lavish love for you, forgiven with an outrageous, extravagant grace that prompts a divine love affair? Do you know that you are exonerated, inhabited and uninhibited?

Ask God to reveal to you any areas that still need His healing touch. Are there places where you are more like Simon, longing for a touch from the Master's heart, desiring to be convinced of this love, but entrenched in defending your image as is?

Do you still feel sometimes like one of the Pharisees with their long lists, long ledgers and long faces? Is your wagging finger loaded and ready to aim and fire?

Do you find yourself at a distance among the other guests? Is your tongue wagging with corrections and criticism of those who are moving closer to the Master?

The best place for our eyes to be fixed in this cast of characters is on Jesus. He is waiting for you to know the deep places of His heart, longing to persuade you of His passion with a beautiful love song. Hear it! He rejoices over you with singing (see Zephaniah 3:17). God the Father is the producer of this song. He paid a big price for you to hear it. God the Son is both the Song and the Singer. The Holy Spirit is His agent. Do you hear it?

Are you sure of the divine Lover who has invited you to the feast? Have you surrendered your entangling chains to run His race with Him? Do you know the ecstasy of the summit? Have you crashed the party that would oppose you and taken the plunge to the depths with Him?

If you have found this place of wholehearted, compelling worship, then your life is being transformed. And, truly, this is what God seeks. As with the Prodigal in the first part of this book, it is not as important that we are home and desiring intimacy as it is that we get to be like our God. Changed. Christlike. It means that He gets to feast with you. He is unencumbered in the marathon of your life. He smiles at your climb up His holy mountain. And He finds delight in diving with you into His unfathomable ways. It is about the look on the Father's face as we cross the finish line.

Will we resemble Him? Will we appear like a poor caricature of Him? Will we altogether remain like ourselves?

Let's learn more about this process of transformation—on moving ahead and continuing in intimacy—in our final chapter.

Searching for More

1. How do you lavish your love on the illegitimate? The divine?
2. Where are you on this continuum?

   InhIbited ——————————————InhAbited

3. How is your worship similar and dissimilar to that of the woman who anointed Jesus?

   W—She *watched, waited* and *went.*
   O —She *offered* what would please His heart.
   R —She was *real.*
   S —Her gift was *sumptuous.*
   H—She was *humble.*
   I —Her response was *immediate.*
   P —She was *persistent.*

12

Transformed in All Dimensions

*M*ark was a strong-willed teenager with a mind of his own and a disrespectful tongue. I know, because I am his mother and I was the target of his caustic words. What bothered his father and me most, though, was his unrepentant spirit. Everything was everyone else's fault. If he got a bad grade in school, it was because the teacher was stupid. If he got in trouble for smoking on school grounds, it did not matter because one of the administrators did it, too. Mediocrity was his hallmark and we were pulling our hair out.

Today Mark is married and the father of his own little boy. His strong will is now godly confidence and his sharp tongue now articulates kindness. Excellence defines his life. God transformed him and he learned repentance. It happened this way.

In Mark's sophomore year his math teacher gave the class a particular assignment. He was to think about what job he would like ten years hence and find a company somewhere in America that offered it. Then he was to write a formal letter of inquiry regarding how employees performing that job use math in their work. Mark had three weeks to complete the assignment. For once he seemed excited about a school project.

Still, one week went by and he had made no effort. As a dutiful parent, I reminded Mark of the due date. His reply was curt: "Get off my case. This is my assignment, not yours."

At the end of the second week, I panicked. *How will he ever get the work done?* I thought. *He's going to fail—again.*

On the day the assignment was due, I noticed a letter sitting on his backpack on the kitchen table. It was written by a young man in our church who was a personal fitness trainer. I knew that Mark was not remotely interested in this job. He had not searched for a company of choice and he had not written a formal letter of request. He had taken the easy way out. *Mediocrity.* That was my angry indictment.

God reminded me, however, that I had prayed an important prayer some six months prior. I had asked the Lord if we, as parents, were doing anything to thwart a repentant heart in Mark. The Lord reminded me of His word in Romans 2:4: "God's kindness leads you toward repentance."

This Scripture raised a heartrending question: "Are we not being kind to Mark?" I asked.

The answer came through a rather obscure verse. In Hosea 11:4, God touched the problem with certain wonder: "I led them with cords of human kindness, with ties of love; I lifted the yoke from their neck and bent down to feed them." I was beginning to get the picture. We had *not* shown Mark kindness with our scathing words and pointing fingers. Instead of lifting any yoke off his neck, we were putting a heavier burden on him with our negative spirits. And rather than bending down to feed him, we were starving his spirit.

God sent in the troops: *Marilyn, instead of raising your loaded finger ready with ammunition, is there anything sincere and positive you could say to Mark that would offer him kindness leading to repentance?* I could not think of a thing.

Finally it came to me. I could congratulate him on getting the assignment done on time. So I did just that. Mark had a sheepish look on his face and retorted with these words: "Well, Dad's mad about it."

I replied, "Why do you think Dad is mad?"

With that, he spun around and went into the bathroom to brush his teeth. I could hear him throwing things around and muttering under his breath.

When Mark came back to the kitchen, he said, "I think I know why Dad is mad. It wasn't the best way to do it, was it?" That was the first repentant response we had heard in years.

God turned all of us around that day. Mark actually became a responsible high school student. His name began to appear on the honor roll, and he went on to hold a position of leadership as student government president. This incident is what our retired pastor George Anderson calls "getting in cahoots with your kids." And with the Lord.

Transformation. It happens all the time. It is God's specialty.

In the last few years I have been honored to get to know a number of people that you might not think would have much in common with each other. Among them are a thief, a gossip, an alcoholic, a glutton, a transgendered man, an adulterer, an abused abuser, and a pity partier. And this is what they have in common: They really believed God's message in Romans 12:2 that they could be transformed by the renewing of their minds.

Today the thief shares his belongings and the gossip has turned a critical spirit into intercession. The alcoholic is dry and in recovery, and the glutton is seventy pounds lighter. The transgendered one is gloriously freed and now pleased to take the role of manhood that God assigned to him in the beginning. The adulterer has repented and remains faithful. The abused one has learned of God's unconditional love, and the one given to self-pity finally realized that a cry for a changed heart wins over a plea for relief.

Transformed! I believe God smiles at such metamorphoses. He challenges us to "put off the old" and "put on the new." His Word is replete with stories of those who "once were, but now are." A pivotal verse most of us have memorized one time or another is 2 Corinthians 5:17: "If anyone is in Christ, he is a new creation; the old has gone, the new has come!"

True transformation comes as we seek more of God in every dimension, as we grow in intimacy with Him. But that is not the end. It is an ongoing process. We are pilgrims in this journey of grace, not tourists hitting some high spots and then moving on to something else. It takes effort to sustain our positions of growth and change. And, we need God's grace to maintain what has been attained.

Reasons We Let Go

If transformation is a reality, if it is true that we are new creations in Christ—and I believe it is—then why is it that, practically speaking, many followers of Jesus do not continue to grow? Or those who do grow in intimacy gradually let their passion die? Some probably feel hopeless about shedding bad habits and questionable character traits. Some are still in bondage and not set free to be intimate with God. And all around are those who hold truly transformed people of their acquaintance to old ways.

There are many explanations for this failure to continue to move forward, but mostly I think three predominate. I would like to take a look at these so that the journey can be completed in the eyes of God.

Fear Gets in the Way

The first reason we find our passion fading is because God's power scares us.

Consider the story of the demoniac, told in Luke 8:26–39. This man was naked, homeless, confused, chained and lonely. He lived in the tombs—places of death and stench—and was ruled by a legion of demons. But one day he was touched by God's power. A man named Jesus asked his name and set him free. Overwhelmed with gratitude, he sat at Jesus' feet clothed, sane, transformed. God was in control—even of the howling demons that made the man a scary legend.

But what was the reaction of the crowds? Luke 8:35 reports that "the people went out to see what had happened. When they came to Jesus, they found the man from whom the demons had gone out, sitting at Jesus' feet, dressed and in his right mind; and they were afraid."

Afraid? *Afraid?* I think it ought to say that "they rejoiced" or "they were astonished." Anything but afraid. But they were so scared they asked Jesus to leave (see Luke 8:37).

Why does God's transforming power induce fear? Perhaps because it goes beyond understanding or because it requires humility—owning up to deficiencies. Or maybe because it demands willingness or giving up control. Or perhaps those who hold back do not really believe God is that passionately in love with them; it is too good to be true. Or maybe they know that obedience is necessary for a miracle and obedience is costly.

Those who hold back watch from a distance, perhaps with yearning. It is safe to embrace the idea in fairy tales; ask Ebenezer Scrooge or Cinderella. The hesitant even applaud Bible accounts. Saul, a persecutor of the Church, turned into Paul, a pillar of the Church. John Mark, the missionary dropout, turned into Mark, the valuable coworker and gospel writer. Joseph, the spoiled little brother, changed into Pharaoh's responsible aide and saved many lives. Moses turned from a temporal thinker into an eternal thinker. Manasseh changed from a proud king to one who humbled himself before the true King. Lazarus was a dead man walking.

Picture the transformation in Frederick Buechner's paraphrase of Jesus' words to the disciples of John the Baptist (see Matthew 11:4–5):

> You go tell John what you've seen around here. Tell him there are people who have sold their seeing-eye dogs and taken up bird-watching. Tell him there are people who've traded in aluminum walkers for hiking boots. Tell him the down and out have turned into the up and coming and a lot of deadbeats are living it up for the first time in their lives.

So what does this mean for us as we seek the wider, higher, longer and deeper dimensions of God's love? It means that we must be in the world but not of the world (see John 17:14–18). We have tasted intimacy; we must never again settle for the status quo. We must choose to face our fears head-on and banish the unbelief they harbor. When we determine to move in the four dimensions of intimacy with God, when we choose *more* and continue to opt for *more*, our transformation has resurrection power behind it. We will never be the same.

In *The Jesus I Never Knew* (Zondervan, 1995), Philip Yancey says that "the Resurrection is the epicenter of belief." That is power coming from the depths of God's love and surfacing at Golgotha. You are closest to the power when you are closest to Him and only He can transform. "Nothing is impossible with God" (Luke 1:37)!

Resurrection power gives us the moxie to dare offer our known, and as yet unknown, deficiencies to the God who came to "proclaim freedom for the captives" and to bestow "a crown of beauty instead of ashes" (Isaiah 61:1, 3). He is sufficient for what is lacking in us. In short, we need His power not only to undergo transformation, but to maintain it.

The apostle Paul says:

> The Lord is the Spirit, and where the Spirit of the Lord is, there is freedom. And we, who with unveiled faces all reflect the Lord's glory, are being transformed into his likeness with ever-increasing glory, which comes from the Lord, who is the Spirit.
>
> 2 Corinthians 3:17–18

Allow me to place those two verses under the microscope. Who is the author of transformation? None other than the Holy Spirit. Whom is this transformation available to? Everyone. Is the change a process or an event? The words *being transformed* indicate an ongoing process. What are we to be transformed into? His likeness. What happens with His glory? We reflect it and increase in it as we are transformed into His likeness. What helps us have unveiled faces? It is the freedom that the Holy Spirit gives.

Eugene Peterson notes in *The Message* (NavPress, 2002) that "one of the stubbornly enduring habits of the human race is to insist on domesticating God. We try to reduce God to a size that conveniently fits our plans and ambitions and tastes." It is one of the ways we evade Him or a sly manner of asking Him to leave.

Our passion for more demands that we stop trying to tame God. We must live on His terms. It is time.

Those who choose not to explore the dimensions of His love out of fear are not unlike the babes in the faith Paul mentions who still require milk and not solid food (see Hebrews 5:11–14). A baby gives an apt picture of the self-absorbed flesh, fearful of change; it likes to be noticed, be stroked and have every need met. The flesh wants to be magnified as the center of all. It wants to be fed only what it likes to eat and then burped and then comforted. It wants to be tucked in, safe and sound, and it wants it now.

The Spirit, however, desires Jesus to be noticed, applauded and magnified—the hub of all. He wants Jesus to bask in the glory He deserves. When we seek more of Him, our fears fall along behind us. Safety defers to the daring pursuit of holiness. And it is about God's timing, not ours.

Old Patterns Prevail

The second main reason some fail to keep moving into deeper dimensions of God's love is because they never really let go of old patterns of thought. This is what I call "pillow-tag theology."

Have you ever fought the pillow-tag battle? These tags stick out of pillowcases on well-made beds like defiant tongues. One day I decided to pull one off. It seemed like a reasonable idea until I noticed the warning printed in bold letters across its face: DO NOT REMOVE UNDER PENALTY OF LAW.

I thought, *I dare not take it off. What if the pillow-tag police knock on my door to search for evidence of my noncompliance?*

Then it occurred to me. I was now the legal owner of that pillow. I paid good money for it. I could do what I wanted to with all parts of it—even the tag. So I ripped it off with relish.

Do you see the parallel? Sometimes even we who are transformed fall back into the flesh and operate as if we have an obligation to live according to our sin natures, like leaving pesky pillow tags in place because we think we have to. But God paid a high price for our freedom with the blood of His one and only Son. We do not have to live according to the flesh. We can live filled with the Holy Spirit.

> Through Christ Jesus the law of the Spirit of life set me free from the law of sin and death. . . . Therefore, brothers, we have an obligation—but it is not to the sinful nature, to live according to it. For if you live according to the sinful nature, you will die; but if by the Spirit you put to death the misdeeds of the body, you will live, because those who are led by the Spirit of God are sons of God.
>
> Romans 8:2, 12–14

Meddling "Resisters"

There are others who fail to maintain transformation because they succumb to the resistance around them. Look at the "resisters" who were at work to destroy the faith of the early believers and the work of the Holy Spirit.

Acts 6–7 tells the story of Stephen, a martyr of the early Church. He was one of seven men chosen for the distribution of food to widows. The search committee had two prerequisites. They needed men "known to be full of the Spirit and wisdom" (Acts 6:3). And this was for the cafeteria line.

It takes a man full of the Holy Spirit to recognize those who resist the Holy Spirit, so it should not surprise us that Stephen saw through the self-righteousness of the Sanhedrin. This was his scathing assessment:

> "You stiff-necked people, with uncircumcised hearts and ears! You are just like your fathers: You always resist the Holy Spirit! Was there ever a prophet your fathers did not persecute? They even killed those who predicted the coming of the Righteous One. And now you have betrayed and murdered him—you who have received the law that was put into effect through angels but have not obeyed it."
>
> Acts 7:51–53

What are some characteristics of those who resist the Holy Spirit? They are stubborn and fleshly. They process what they hear through calloused hearts (see Isaiah 6:9–10). They are not surrendered and are unwilling for transformation. They follow faulty tradition and usually persecute any messenger who delivers a message that does not agree with their own desires.

Acts 7:54 records the predictable response of these ecclesiastical leaders: "They were furious." They "gnashed their teeth" at Stephen. I have always wondered how that looks. Do gnashers bare their teeth like grizzlies or do they grind their jaws together audibly? Either way, it demonstrates disapproval. They "dragged him out of the city and began to stone him" (verse 58).

Acts 7:58 says that some witnesses "laid their clothes at the feet of a young man named Saul." Why? Because they wanted to pick up their own stones unencumbered. Why Saul? Because they knew he sympathized with their misguided cause.

Contrast the pictures of Stephen and Saul. Stephen, full of the Holy Spirit, looked to heaven. Saul, a leader in the resistance, saw heaven flash down around him (see Acts 9:3). Stephen saw the glory of God (see Acts 7:55–56). Saul counted on the glory of man (see Philippians 3:4–6). Stephen was persecuted. Saul was a persecutor. Stephen served the Lord. Saul persecuted the Lord (see Acts 9:4). Stephen saw the Lord (see Acts 7:55–56). Saul was temporarily blinded by the Lord (see Acts 9:8–9). Full of forgiveness, Stephen prayed for his hateful persecutors: "Lord, do not hold this sin against them" (Acts 7:60). "Saul was there, giving approval to his death" (Acts 8:1).

Do you see how important it is to understand the obstacles resisters will put in your path as you grow in intimacy with God? Not only do those obstacles work for the death of Spirit-filled living, they will result eventually in persecution, a scattering of God's people, destruction and bondage. Acts 8:1 states: "On that day a great persecution broke out against the church at Jerusalem, and all except the apostles were scattered throughout Judea and Samaria." Acts 8:3 says that "Saul began to destroy the church. Going from house to house, he dragged off men and women and put them in prison." What were the godly men in that place doing, you might ask? Acts 8:2 says they "buried Stephen and mourned deeply for him."

Are resisters in your life thwarting your pursuit of intimacy? Do they keep you from going forward? Are you mourning the death of anything Spirit-filled in your life? Or might you be a resister?

In the next chapter of Acts we see a very different picture of Saul. Suddenly he "began to preach in the synagogues that Jesus is the Son of God" (Acts 9:20). That is quite a transformation! What happened? God got Saul's attention on the road to Damascus and sent Ananias to him with a message: "Brother Saul, the Lord—Jesus, who appeared to you on the road as you were coming here—has sent me so that you may see again and be filled with the Holy Spirit" (Acts 9:17). Because of the faithful witness of those who maintained intimacy with their Savior at any cost, the Gospel spread and more lives were transformed for the glory of God.

Moving into More

My experience in this process of growing in the four dimensions of God's love has come with surrender to the Holy Spirit. He has stirred in my heart five God-directed prayers. You have already read about some of them. They are: (1) convince me of Your love; (2) set my spirit free; (3) draw me close; (4) expose my flesh; and (5) help me maintain what has been attained by Your grace. These prayers are not meant to be a formula for you to follow, but a sample of the questions you might ask God about your own needs.

Surprisingly, God's longings for us are all wrapped up in these five prayers. Remember when we were on the mountain of God and going higher with Him there? It was at the summit that His longings were revealed: freedom, connection, treasure, priesthood and holiness. As I ask, *Convince me of Your love*, He reveals His desire for me to be assured that I am His treasure. In the utterance of *Set my spirit free*, He offers liberty. As I say *draw me close*, He exposes His grand scheme for connection. In my prayer to *expose my flesh*, He reveals His holiness. And as I ask Him to *maintain what has been attained*, He shows that He has given me a priesthood ministry. I did not know that was happening. It is one of the wonders of *more*.

The transformations He has brought to me over the past several years are products of the crucible. I would like to challenge you to ask God about some of these possible changes for your life as you continue to seek more of Him.

1. Might He want to change you from a diligent student of the Word to a careful listener of the "Word made flesh"? (After listening and study, get counsel to confirm that what you think you heard does not contradict the written revelation.)
2. Would He want to move you from one who prays to Him to one who longs to pray with Him? (You can accomplish that by asking Him to incline your heart to pray what our great High Priest and intercessor, as described in Hebrews 7:25–26, is already praying.)
3. Might God want to transform your desire for the approval of others to a desire, above all else, for His approval?
4. Would you consider allowing Him to move your heart from activity for Him to adoration of Him? This is not an either/or matter, but one of priority.
5. If you are a Bible teacher, would you consider letting Him help you go from finding your identity as a teacher of the Word to hardly believing you get to touch it?
6. Might you allow Him to change you from wanting to speak your mind to longing for others to hear His voice?
7. Would you consider letting Him transform a heart impressed with what you have done for Him to a heart awed with what He dares to do through you?
8. Might you become concerned about the longings of His heart rather than the desires of your own?

9. Are there ways you try to harness God to your vision rather than pray for Jesus to be your vision?

10. Might you look more for His face than His hands?

11. Will you surrender areas of bondage, or at least ask Him about them?

12. Instead of just glances in His direction, will you yearn to gaze longingly at God?

13. Would you go from presuming upon people to really desiring to love them—especially those who cannot give you anything in return?

14. Will you allow Him to move you from speaking more to listening more?

15. From furtive anxiety to a grateful, petitioning heart filling with peace?

16. From intellectually knowing "God is love" to being convinced that He passionately loves you?

17. From telling to asking God?

18. From demanding answers to responding to His questions?

19. Will you allow Him to turn your impatience with people to more surrender of your expectations—your standard—for people?

20. Will you allow Him to move you from duty in the disciplines of the faith to delight in the God of the faith? (Then your passion will draw you to the disciplines.)

21. Will you turn from displeasure in the hard places in the pilgrimage to joy in the journey?

22. From defending your image to humbling yourself before God and man?

23. From thinking that it is "Christ *and* you, the hope of glory" to realizing that it is indeed "Christ *in* you, the hope of glory"?

I am humbled looking at the list and mindful of my many rough edges that need His touch. But day by day intimacy grows, until that glorious day when "we shall be like him, for we shall see him as he is" (1 John 3:2). In the meantime, I believe the God who draws us whispers these words to my heart—and yours:

> I am the Transformer. For from Me and through Me and to Me are all things. I want you to be like My Son: single-minded, with prayer as a priority. I want you to follow His example—one who is intimate with Me, an eternal thinker, cloaked in humility, forgiving, alive and joyful. I desire that you know what is in man and love him anyway.
>
> You can change through surrender. My mercies assure it. Therefore, in view of My mercy, offer your bodies as living sacrifices, holy and pleasing to God—this is your spiritual act of worship.
>
> The process of transformation is in how you think. Do not be conformed any longer to the pattern of this world, but be transformed by the renewing of your mind. (See Romans 11:33–12:2.)

And I believe it would please Him to remind us that in seeking more, we are giving glory to God in the living of His will—"his good, pleasing and perfect will" (Romans 12:2).

God's love is wide and long and high and deep. You have gone wider. He has offered the richest of fare and you have traded crumbs for caviar. You have gone longer. You have reached out to Him as He has been walking on water toward you. He has been the glory and the lifter of your head as you have gone higher. And now you have gone deeper, too, and found that underneath are His everlasting arms.

You have taken hold of that for which Christ Jesus has taken hold of you. May you continue to be filled to the measure of all His fullness. Nothing held back. We dare not settle for more of anything other than more of Him. What a great gift, this surrender, this humility, this brokenness—all of this that offers us more of Him! Press on. There is more!

"Now to him who is able to do immeasurably more than all we ask or imagine, according to his power that is at work within us, to him be glory in the church and in Christ Jesus throughout all generations, for ever and ever! Amen" (Ephesians 3:20–21).

Searching for More

1. Of the reasons given below that could explain our struggle in grasping transformation, which two most apply to you? Ask God why.

    _____ Fear of the unknown
    _____ It is beyond our ability to comprehend
    _____ Pride
    _____ Loss of control
    _____ God's passion is too lavish
    _____ Obedience is costly
    _____ Unbelief
    _____ Other

2. Which of the biblical examples of transformation speaks most to your heart? Why?

    _____ Paul: persecutor to pillar (see Acts 9:1–22)
    _____ Joseph: boastful to generous (see Genesis 37–50)
    _____ Sinful woman: lover of the illegitimate to lover of the divine (see Luke 7:36–50)

_____ John Mark: missionary dropout to
valued coworker and gospel writer (see
2 Timothy 4:11)

_____ Moses: temporal thinker to eternal
thinker (see Acts 7:20–38)

_____ Manasseh: proud king to humble servant
(see 2 Kings 21:1–18; 2 Chronicles
33:1–20)

_____ The Prodigal in Jesus' parable: rebellious
ingrate to grateful son (see Luke
15:11–32)

_____ Lazarus: a man called from death to life
(see John 11:1–44)

3. In the list of ways to be like Jesus, below, which do
you think you need most?

_____ Making prayer your priority

_____ Being single-minded

_____ Growing in intimacy with the Father

_____ Being an "eternal thinker"

_____ Having no self-pity

_____ Seeking humility in service

_____ Living in joy

_____ Forgiving your enemies

_____ Knowing what is in man and still loving

4. Are you full of the Holy Spirit or resistant to the Holy
Spirit? Go to Him in prayer about that.

Appendix 1

God's Favorite Word: "Come!"

Scripture	How He Says It	Whom He Says It To	Results	Revelation of Him	The Surrender
Matthew 11:28–30	"Come to me"	The tired and weary	Rest	I AM	Take His yoke and learn
James 4:8	"Come near"	Those at a distance	He comes near to us	The gate	Holiness: Seek no other door
Matthew 4:19–20	"Come, follow me"	Those who do things their way	He makes us leaders for His way	The way	Leave our familiar "nets"
John 11:43	"Come out!"	Those dead in their spirits	Freedom and life	Resurrection and the life	Choose life, not death
Isaiah 1:18	"Come now, let us reason together"	Sinners	Purity and cleansing	The refiner's fire	Reason with Him, not alone
John 7:37–39	"Come to me and drink"	Thirsty	Overflow with the Spirit	The living water	Seek no other water

Scripture	How He Says It	Whom He Says It To	Results	Revelation of Him	The Surrender
Revelation 4:1	"Come up here"	Those wanting to know more of Him	Revelation of Him	The truth	Leave the horizontal for the vertical
Isaiah 50:8, NASB	"[Come, you] who [have] a case against Me"	Those angry with God	Honesty face-to-face with God	The light of the world	Repent
John 21:12	"Come and have breakfast"	Those hungry for Him	Filled by His feeding	The bread of life	Desire no other food
Psalm 34:11	"Come ... listen"	Those with stopped-up ears	Knowing the fear of God	The life	Stop speaking
Song of Songs 2:10, 13	"Come with me"	Those who want to be with Him	Intimacy	The lover of our souls	Hold nothing back
Luke 19:5	"Come down immediately"	Those who want to see Him	Transformation	The transformer	Leave our high places

Appendix 2

The Ten Commandments from the Lover of Our Souls

1. I want you to allow Me to be your first love. (Have no other gods before Me.)
2. I want you to allow Me to be your only true love. (Honor no idols.)
3. I want My name to be sweet on your lips. (Don't take My name in vain.)
4. I want you to make "our date day" together really special. (Keep the Sabbath.)
5. I want you to rejoice over your parentage as I do, even if it is/was difficult. (Honor your parents.)
6. I want you to savor life as I do. (Do not commit murder.)
7. I want you to desire Me over the desires of your flesh. (Don't commit adultery.)
8. I want you to allow Me to provide what you need. (Don't steal.)
9. I want you to convince those around you that they are my treasured possession by being careful with your words. (Give no false testimony.)
10. I want you to want only the belongings we have together. (Don't covet.)

Marilyn N. Anderes became a child of God in 1972. Married to John for forty years, she is the mother of three and the grandmother of six. She is a graduate of the University of Wisconsin and has taught Bible studies and led women's retreats and seminars for the last 25 years. Marilyn has served as a mentor and Bible teacher for wives of NBA players in the Washington, D.C., area.

She is a contributing editor at *Good News* magazine, writing the column "From the Heart." Articles from her pen have appeared in such periodicals as *Decision* magazine and *Discipleship Journal*. She has also authored *A Workshop on Self-Giving*, *The Great Encourager* and *From the Heart of the Word*.

Marilyn yearns to live the longings of God's heart and to help others see more of Him. On any given day you can find her worshiping God at the piano, applauding Him over yet another wonder in His Word and offering laughter and love to those with whom she shares His message of transformation.